R Is For Rainbow

Developing Young Children's Thinking Skills Through The Alphabet

Sandra Anselmo
Pamela Rollins
Rita Schuckman

Addison-Wesley Publishing Company

Menlo Park, California · Reading, Massachusetts
Wokingham, Berkshire, U.K. · Amsterdam · Don Mills, Ontario · Sydney

ABOUT THE AUTHORS

Sandra Anselmo *is an associate professor in the School of Education at the University of the Pacific, Stockton, California. She has taught and administered early childhood programs in various parts of the United States. Dr. Anselmo is now a nationally recognized teacher, author, and consultant on issues concerning the education and development of young children.*

Rita Schuckman *and* **Pamela Rollins** *founded Rainbow School in Stockton in 1978. Their school offers a preschool program, a kindergarten, and an enrichment experience program for primary students. They have served as consultants to school districts and corporations on early childhood curriculum and administration. All three authors are parents of children who have developed their thinking skills through the alphabet program at Rainbow School.*

This book is published by the Addison-Wesley Innovative Division.

Design: Detta Penna
Illustrations: Jane McCreary
Photographs: Sandra Anselmo
Cover photograph provided expressly for the publisher by Wayland Lee, Addison-Wesley
Publishing Company, Inc.

ISBN-0-201-20199-2
EFG-AL-898

Contents

Letters

Using the *R Is for Rainbow* Alphabet Program

Who should use this program?

Preschool, kindergarten, and first grade teachers should use this alphabet program if they have the following goals:

Developing language skills

Teaching sound-symbol associations

Developing thinking skills in an orderly sequence

Comprehension

Memory

Decision making

Problem solving and following directions (convergent production)

Creativity (divergent production)

Developing eye-hand coordination and small-muscle skills

Developing concepts about print

What is a sound?

What is a letter?

What is a word?

Where do we start reading?

In which direction do we read?

Using multisensory materials and all major modalities

Integrating various curricular components into a unified program

Creating feelings of success

Parents and teachers of English as a second language (ESL) could also adapt the program for their use.

The Goals of the Program

Our preschool-primary program seeks to achieve all of the ambitious goals set forth above, and the alphabet program provides an integrated vehicle for doing so. We start with *A,* end with *Z,* and take a unique and innovative journey in between. Perhaps the best way to begin explaining that journey is to describe how we implement each goal.

Developing Language Skills

We believe that language development provides the foundation for literacy. In all parts of our alphabet program, we try to elicit descriptive, expressive language from children. We ask them to tell us about objects that they bring from home and about ideas that they use in school activities and projects. We work together to dramatize concepts such as under/over and up/down so that children will have meaningful operational definitions. We make conscious choices about our language patterns, depending upon the thinking patterns that we want children to use. For instance, to encourage decision making, we avoid questions that result in "yes" or "no" responses in favor of those that require children's evaluations and explanations.

Reading to children promotes language development. As part of our alphabet program, we have selected both classic and current literature that relates to each letter and contributes to children's understanding of themselves and their world. Children then talk with us and with each other about the ideas, concepts, characters, events, and descriptive language. Sometimes we follow the reading of a favorite book with our own production of a play in which children develop the dialogue and action. The results can be exciting.

In our program, children also have frequent opportunities to create original stories. Children dictate or write stories about their wishes, ideas, or experiences. These stories are often read to the entire group. A supportive climate is maintained when experience stories are shared: All contributions are shown respect and interest. Children, like all authors, find affirmation in hearing supportive comments from peers about their words and the underlying ideas.

Teaching Sound-Symbol Associations

The program introduces one letter at a time, beginning with *A* and continuing through the alphabet in sequence, although it would be possible to devise another order. Our guiding principle has been to surround children with sound-symbol associations that are tied to concrete objects and meaningful experiences. The theory of Jean Piaget has helped us to be aware of the tendency of young children to view the world from their own unique perspectives. We have therefore used many approaches in presenting each sound-symbol association in order to maximize the probability that one or more will be processed by each child. We seek to surround children with sound-symbol associations in much the same way that we surrounded them with language when they were first learning to speak.

Reviews of recent research justify the importance of letter-name and letter-sound instruction in preparation for formal reading instruction. It has been found that the main learning difficulty demonstrated by young children is associating letter names or sounds with their symbols. Learning these associations takes a great deal of time for most young children. An alphabet program such as ours follows the procedures recommended by reading researchers: teaching sound-symbol associations gradually and meaningfully over the course of the year or two before formal reading instruction is introduced.

Sound-symbol associations are presented with an understanding of the great variability of development within any group of children. Although children are surrounded by sound-symbol associations, these associations are not forced on them. Children can succeed and feel good about the components of the program—the daily large group, small group, and individual activities—without seeing the Gestalt or pattern to the entire alphabet program. Eventually, though, because of the pervasiveness of the program, there comes a time when children say "A-ha!" about their personal discovery of the pattern of sound-symbol associations. The breakthrough may be at *A* or not until *Z,* but thoughtful use of this alphabet program does lead to these understandings—an important first step in literacy. As one four-year-old exclaimed with a great sense of joy, "Everything begins with something!"

In presenting sound-symbol associations, we make children aware that some letters have more than one sound. The "sound test" is frequently given to objects. The teacher might say, "B-b-b-bear. Does it pass the *B* test?" In the case of vowels or less consistent consonants, we emphasize one sound but explain that just as David is sometimes called Davey or Dave, letters sometimes have other sounds. English is a highly nonphonetic language, and we recommend making children aware of the

variability at the outset rather than misleading them into thinking that sound-symbol associations are consistent.

Developing Thinking Skills in an Orderly Sequence

The theoretical bases of the program are Jean Piaget's theory of intellectual development and the Structure of Intellect (SOI) theory developed by J. P. Guilford and elaborated upon by Mary Meeker. These theories have helped us to understand children's thinking processes and have assisted us in developing children's thinking skills in a systematic way through interaction.

Jean Piaget's theory describes a sequence of stages through which all children pass. According to Piaget, most preschool and primary grade children are at a prelogical level of thinking. They tend to see the world mainly from their own perspectives and to learn best from hands-on experiences.

In developing projects relating to each letter in the alphabet, we have been careful to heed the lessons inherent in Piaget's work. We have related the activities to the children's lives and interests as closely as possible, encouraged home-school interactions, presented each concept in a variety of ways, and made sure that children are encouraged to use all of their senses.

The SOI theory identifies five different thinking operations: (1) comprehension, (2) memory, (3) decision making, (4) problem solving (including following directions), and (5) creativity. The first three of these thinking operations are foundations for the last two: Children must first comprehend, next remember, and then be able to make decisions in order to use more complex problem solving strategies and creativity.

For each letter of the alphabet, we have devised activities that develop all five of these SOI thinking operations, emphasizing the first three. Comprehension is strengthened by multisensory experiences—seeing, hearing, touching, smelling, tasting—and by the accompanying explanations of relationships within, between, and among experiences. Memory training, a cornerstone of the program because of its importance as a foundation for later academic and life success, is conducted with games, such as concentration, and activities, such as the memory book (described later). Experiences in decision making pervade the program; opportunities range from selecting the color of paper for a project to classifying objects according to a consistent criterion. Skills in problem solving and following directions are developed through multisensory letter projects, food projects, and other projects. Creativity is supported throughout the program by the respect given to children and their thoughts and ideas; more specific nurturing of creativity is found in activities such as brainstorming, creative dramatics, and creative writing. All of these activities are described more fully later in the book, and the SOI theory is explained in more detail in the Appendix.

Developing Eye-Hand Coordination and Small-Muscle Skills

The multisensory letter projects in our alphabet program have been designed to develop eye-hand coordination and small-muscle skills sequentially. For instance, the early projects do not presuppose that children are able to use scissors; rather, through the projects, children are gradually introduced to handling scissors. At first children only snip rectangles or squares from precut strips of construction paper. Wider or narrower strips of paper are made available, depending on individual skill. As children become successful with snipping, they begin to cut around outlines. All the patterns in this book have simple contours to facilitate successful cutting experiences.

Eye-hand coordination and small-muscle skills are developed throughout the program in other ways, too. Food projects, science experiences, projects to develop thinking skills, and fingerplays all contribute to children's abilities to manipulate objects.

Developing Concepts About Print

As part of our alphabet program, we directly teach the terminology of reading instruction, called "concepts about print" in the reading research literature. Research has shown that young children do not know what teachers are talking about when terms such as *sound, letter,* or *word* are used. Researchers recommend that the meanings of these terms be taught directly, so that children and teachers will have a common vocabulary when formal reading instruction begins. In order to introduce these terms in meaningful ways, we consciously use them as we help children to write experience stories, as we read aloud, and as we conduct other parts of the program. We explain the spaces that separate words, the punctuation that appears, the pattern of upper and lower case letters, where we start to read in a book and on a page, in which direction we read, and any other features of printed language that interest the children. Our instruction occurs in the natural flow of other language and thinking activities and is an important aspect of the program.

Using Multisensory Materials and All Major Modalities

Each sound-symbol association is presented through many senses. For example, the teacher and children might write the letter in the air with imaginary crayons while saying the sound. Or partners might take turns forming the letter on each others' backs with a finger, an empty roll-on deodorant container, or a vegetable brush. Or, working on the multisensory letter projects, children might be encouraged to look at, feel, and trace the letter while saying the sound.

Throughout the program, children have many other chances to sharpen all of their senses. For each letter of the alphabet, we have designed comprehension projects that require use of the three major modalities: visual, auditory, and tactile-kinesthetic. These projects provide opportunities for children to explore aspects of the environment by looking, listening, and touching. Sometimes, as in food projects, the sensory dimensions of tasting and smelling are added.

Integrating Various Curricular Components into a Unified Program

Our alphabet program is designed to form the core of the curriculum for preschool, kindergarten, or first grade classes. We want teachers to feel free to add their own creative embellishments, but the program has sufficient depth, breadth, and variety for teachers to feel good about using it without supplements.

In addition to building the development of language, reading, thinking, perceptual-motor, sensory, and other skills into the curriculum, we specifically suggest food projects, art projects, science projects, and music activities for each letter of the alphabet. Mathematical experiences for each letter are supplied predominantly under the heading of decision making as a thinking skill. These mathematical experiences involve children in observing, comparing, contrasting, sequencing, classifying, making patterns, and measuring. For each letter, we also list possible field trips and visitors to allow children to become acquainted with typical community resources. (Most of the field trips can be adapted to in-class experiences if children are unable to take field trips. For example, instead of visiting the barber for *B,* a barber could be invited to visit class and perhaps give someone a haircut—with advance parental permission, of course.) Other social studies activities are suggested under comprehension as a thinking skill (for instance, study of the family for *F* and of the neighborhood for *N*). The curriculum is a rich one, unified around each of the twenty-six letters of the alphabet.

Creating Feelings of Success

We who work with young children must assume responsibility for the image of themselves that they see in our eyes. During the years spent developing and using this program, we have always kept in mind the critical importance of positive self-concept in education. In nurturing children's positive feelings, we have learned to become aware of what we do and say and how we do and say it.

This program yields an abundance of opportunities and experiences that can be handled with success at many different levels by children who each have a unique time-table of development. Our responsibility in using this program is to cherish and celebrate each bit of growth from each special child. As children note their growth and see our genuine joy, they develop confidence in themselves as learners and thinkers. They *feel* successful and they *are* successful.

Procedures

The purpose of this book is to share information about the alphabet program that we have developed. The alphabet program is started after we have become acquainted with the children's needs and interests—three or four weeks into the school year. From that point on, we use a wide variety of activities to introduce one letter each week, except for short weeks and weeks with major holidays. Before we describe these alphabet activities, some general procedures and materials that we use regularly will be outlined.

Grouping

We typically begin the day with a large group time, during which children share objects from home that begin with the letter of the week. Children spend the majority of the rest of the day rotating among interest centers. The multisensory letter projects, food projects, science projects, experience stories, and other projects are usually conducted with small groups of children during the part of the day devoted to interest centers. The day then ends with another group time at which we sing, do fingerplays, and read.

The combination of large and small group times works effectively for us. But, knowing that small groups might be unrealistic in some settings, we have developed activities that can be adapted for use with groups of varying sizes.

Bulletin Board

We fill a prominent bulletin board with upper and lower case representations of the letter of the week and many colorful pictures of things that begin with that letter. Under the bulletin board is a table for objects whose names begin with that letter.

Letter Bag

When children come to school, they immediately deposit objects from home in the letter bag for

The Letter Bag: *G* for Grizzly Bear

sharing at group time. (The twenty-six letter bags have drawstring tops and block letters on the sides.) Communication at home is facilitated by parents and children searching together for appropriate objects to share at school. Communication at school is encouraged as children come to the front of the group to tell what they brought, how it is used, whose it is, etc. Teachers maintain a supportive climate during letter bag time: All contributions and contributors are shown respect and interest. After sharing, objects are placed on the table for a closer look during the week. At the end of the week, children take their contributions home.

We also make a school collection of small objects for each letter. This permanent collection is stored in twenty-six labeled boxes or bags. Of the many uses for the school collection, the following are the most important: (1) classification by beginning sound when objects from two or more boxes are mixed, and (2) memory activities in which children study a grouping and then identify which object has been removed.

As an alternative to bringing objects from home for the letter bag, children can be asked to draw or cut out pictures of objects. At the end of the week, the pictures can be mounted on a large piece of poster board.

Golden Letters

Each week, block letters covered with golden glitter are provided for each child whose first name begins with the letter of the week. At group times these children wear the golden letters on yarn around their necks and receive special attention. Positive self-concept soars, and everyone can look forward to a turn. (Sometimes figuring out when that turn will be brings about a discovery about sequencing.) We include patterns for the golden letters.

Food Projects

At least once every week, during the time children are free to rotate among interest centers, they participate in a food project that begins with or relates to the letter of the week. The single portion method is used frequently, and many recipes are from *Cook and Learn* by Bev Vietch and Thelma Harms (Addison-Wesley, 1981). Usually the food project is eaten on the same day that it is prepared.

Multisensory Letter Projects

On different days during the week, children complete at least two multisensory letter projects. One of these projects involves the upper-case letter and the other the lower-case letter of the week. These projects are designed to involve the senses: most projects use visual, auditory, and tactile-kinesthetic modalities. For example, the lower-case *a* can be printed on an apple shape. The letter form is then covered by the children with squares that they snip from construction paper strips. Children look at, feel, and trace the letter as they work at the cutting activity. Then the teacher says, "*a . . . apple*" and writes it on the completed project. Sometimes

the children are asked if they can remember any other things that begin with the sound; if they do, words that reflect their interests are written down also.

The multisensory letter projects predominantly develop convergent thinking skills and the ability to follow directions. But, even so, children are purposely given many choices within the established structure of the projects. For instance, they may select the color of the paper or material to be glued, and they are always encouraged to add any desired embellishments.

Tasting Parties

Another of the comprehension activities that we use regularly is called a tasting party. We gather together foods that relate to the letter of the week, and children observe, smell, taste, describe, and compare them. For *D* week, for instance, we set up a tray of dairy products, which includes the following: milk, cheeses, plain yogurt, flavored yogurt, cottage cheese, buttermilk, and cream cheese.

Dairy Products Tasting Tray

Children receive cups, spoons, and napkins and sample the various products. Sometimes we ask the children to vote for their favorite product by placing a sticker on a chart. Later we discuss how to read the chart and which product was the preferred.

Note: For all tasting parties, it is assumed that teachers are aware of children with specific allergies.

Memory Book

To improve memory, each week we use a teacher-made memory book. At first, three sections of the memory book are filled with pictures and shown to children for one second per picture. Afterward, children recall as much as they can about the pictures. As children become proficient, additional pictures are added to the memory book until all six sections are filled.

Making a Memory Book

You need:

    Clear acetate
    Poster board
    Plastic tape

To Make Your Memory Book:

1. Cut acetate and poster board into 8½ x 11'' pieces.
2. Cover each piece of poster board with acetate and close on three sides with plastic tape. (The fourth side allows you to put in and remove your memory pictures.)
3. Connect the pieces of acetate-covered poster board with plastic tape, as shown in in the photograph.

Memory Tray

We also develop memory skills by using a memory tray. A memory tray can be as simple as a shoe box with a lid. Items from the letter bag or the school letter collection are put on the tray and shown to the children, and either an object is removed and children try to remember what it is, or the entire collection is hidden and children try to remember what was there. Memory responds well to training, and part of that training can involve using the memory tray each week.

"Magic" Page

Reading books provides another opportunity for memory training. The teacher shows the children a "magic" page before beginning a story. When that page is reached in reading the book, the children who remember it raise their hands quietly. The teacher acknowledges them with a smile and continues with the story.

Visual Closure Cards

Visual closure is the ability to complete in one's head a picture or drawing that is incomplete as shown. Visual closure is a foundational comprehension ability that is necessary in the reading process. Children weak in visual closure often have tracking and word reversal problems, but visual closure can be improved with practice. For this reason, we suggest that visual closure cards be used each week. Patterns for visual closure cards accompany all twenty-six letters of the alphabet.

The patterns for visual closure cards show two versions of each letter and picture. One version (mounted on side one) leaves gaps in the outline. Children are shown side one and asked to be good detectives and to try to figure out what is depicted. After the children have had time to think, the second version (mounted on side two) is shown so that children can verify or modify their responses. Side two shows the entire outline of the object or symbol.

Brainstorming

Brainstorming is an exciting activity that encourages a special kind of creative thinking—fluency, which is the ability to produce a ready flow of ideas. Fluency can be enhanced through experiences with brainstorming.

In brainstorming, children are encouraged to think of many things that fit a given classification. It is usually best to begin with a familiar classification, such as "things that you can see right now." The teacher starts the activity by suggesting possibilities ("I see a clock, a wall, two doors . . .") until the children begin to chime in. All ideas should be accepted with enthusiasm and encouragement.

At first, children will contribute many duplicate responses—*clock* may be given five or six times by different children—but each should be received as positively as the first. As children gain practice with brainstorming, they include more variety in their responses.

After the first few brainstorming sessions, it is interesting to record the children's responses on a chalkboard or wall chart. They are pleased to see how many good ideas that they have had, and they can see that they are becoming more fluent with each session.

Often children want to evaluate ideas when they are suggested. The teacher must be firm in helping children to wait until all the good ideas are given or until the prespecified time limit has arrived. Stopping to evaluate ideas while brainstorming inhibits their flow and makes children self-conscious.

After the brainstorming activity, the entire group can help to make decisions about whether all ideas fit the original classification. If there are disagreements, children can engage in discussion and eventually vote on whether to keep disputed items on the list.

We have developed brainstorming activities relating to many letters of the alphabet. Using them will encourage an important aspect of creativity.

Classifying

A decision-making activity that accompanies each alphabet letter involves classifying objects into groups, according to some kind of logical system. Marbles, buttons, seeds, keys—all of these objects can be grouped according to similarities and differences among them. Classifying is a foundational ability in reading and mathematics, and we provide many opportunities for children to enhance their ability to use this thinking skill.

The earliest classification activities revolve around the meanings of the concepts *same* and *different.* Three buttons might be shown to a group of children; two buttons would be large, one would be small, and all would be the same color to focus attention only on the size variable. The children would be asked to put the two that are alike or the same together. As children show that they thoroughly understand the concepts same/different, more objects can be added to the set to be classified. Gradually, more than one variable can be included, too.

We always ask children to explain their classifications, and we have learned from their justifications. For example, once we had thought of many possi-

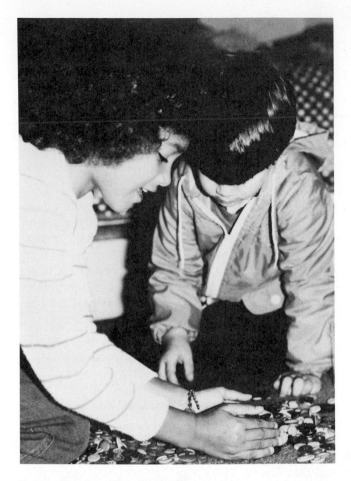

Getting Ready to Classify Buttons

ble ways to classify apples (color, size, shape, markings). A five-year-old seemed to produce only a random arrangement of apples but surprised us with her logical explanation: She had separated the apples with stems from those without stems. We encourage children's creative thinking.

Diagnostic Procedures

Diagnostic procedures are an informal but important part of the alphabet program. We assess children's language and thinking skills as they enter the program and throughout the year as they participate in it. We try to ascertain their strengths, interests, and needs in order to know how best to encourage their optimal development. The alphabet program affords many opportunities to talk with children and to listen sensitively to them, and we make the most of these opportunities. We also create situations that provide us with information about children's language and thinking skills.

We organize our diagnostic procedures around the five thinking skills that are emphasized in the alphabet program: comprehension, memory, decision making, problem solving and following directions, and creativity. We record our findings in the form of narrative observations on Personal Diagnostic Records (See facing page) and place them in the children's files. These records provide a basis for measuring children's growth, reporting that growth to parents, and planning the curriculum.

Comprehension

During the first weeks of school, enrichment and diagnosis precede the introduction of the alphabet program. We review concepts—for instance, color, shape, size, body parts, aspects of familiar environments—and the language associated with these concepts. We give children frequent opportunities to express themselves, and we listen carefully as they do so.

All during the year we show children many sets of picture cards and collections of foods, animals, toys, and other objects. We ask them to tell us what they see and to give us a description. How able are they to talk about color, size, shape, texture, smell, and function?

Memory

We play memory games with small groups of children, beginning at a very fundamental level, and observe their responses. We might put two balls on the floor for description, observation, and handling. Later we might remove the balls and ask children to recall as much as possible about them. Or we might use the memory book, described earlier, with just two or three pictures in it. How much are they able to recall?

Decision Making

We provide children with a small array of objects and ask them to tell us whether they are the same or different and whether they can find two that are alike. If they seem to understand the concept of matching, we ask them if they can put the objects in a group according to a similar characteristic or in a sequence according to size. At other times we ask children to evaluate behavior in real-life situations—"What would you do if you found money on the sidewalk?" What is their understanding of classification, sequence, and personal responsibility?

Problem Solving and Following Directions

We note children's responses to the individual and group instructions that we give. We ask them to copy shapes, draw pictures of themselves and their families, move from one activity to another at times of transition, sit within a certain area at group time, etc. Children are at many different levels of readiness to react to such instructions, and we try to determine how best to reach out to each child. How able are they to follow specific directions?

Creativity

We ask all children to dictate experience stories during the year. They choose an action picture that interests them from a large assortment. We request that they tell us about it, and we record what they say. These language experience stories give us some idea about the fluency, flexibility, and richness of children's language and concepts. How creative are they in their use of language?

Communicating with Parents

Parents are the first teachers of their children, and their influence has a continuity unmatched by that of other teachers. Much of the learning in the home situation takes place spontaneously, but if parents understand the goals of the classroom program, they can also create opportunities to strengthen concepts presented at school. We communicate frequently with parents—by means of letters, meetings, and conferences—so that they understand what we are trying to do and how they can help and so that we understand them and their children better. We strive to form a partnership between home and school.

The letter on page xiv introduces parents to the goals of the alphabet program. Parents are invited to attend a meeting at which we demonstrate activities and materials and talk more about how they can extend the excitement of the alphabet program into their homes.

Personal Diagnostic Record

Name: _____   Birthdate: _____

I. Comprehension

Date	Object Shown	Descriptive language used	Comments

II. Memory

Date	Object Shown	Details remembered	Comments

III. Decision Making

Date	Situation Presented	Assessment of situation	Comments

IV. Problem Solving and Following Directions

Date	Situation Presented	Response to situation	Comments

V. Creativity

Date	Opportunity Presented	Response to opportunity	Comments

SAMPLE INTRODUCTORY LETTER TO PARENTS

Dear Parents,

Your child will be experiencing an exciting alphabet program this year. This alphabet program is designed to help your child to achieve the following important goals:

To develop language skills and fluency
To learn relationships between sounds and letters;
To develop thinking skills, such as comprehension, memory, decision making, problem solving and following directions, and creativity
To develop coordination of eyes with hands and skill in using small muscles
To develop concepts about sounds, words, letters, and how books are organized
To use all senses in exploring the environment
To feel successful

This alphabet program has been built on a foundation of recent research about how young children learn to read.

In these first weeks we have become acquainted with your child's strengths, interests, and needs. What we have learned about your child will guide us when we begin the alphabet program next week. We start with the letter *A* and continue sequentially in the following weeks until we end the alphabet program at *Z*.

Next week and throughout the year, you can reinforce your child's learning at home. Children will be encouraged to bring to school items and pictures that have the letter of the week as the beginning sound. Items and pictures will be placed in the letter bag when children arrive at school and then shared with others at group time. You can participate in your child's search for items and pictures for the letter bag and help your child decide whether what has been selected does indeed begin with the letter of the week. Do not worry, however, if your child wants to bring items for the letter bag that start with some other letter; at school we will gradually and positively guide children toward being able to make these difficult discriminations.

Each Monday we will introduce the sound and shape of the letter of the week. Your child's understanding of that letter will be strengthened by our careful selection of activities. For instance, for *B* week, here are some typical choices: banana bread and butter for food projects; bat and bear for multisensory letter projects; blotto prints and bark rubbings for art projects; separating beans into groups for a thinking game; *Brown Bear, Brown Bear* for the story; ''Bunny'' for fingerplay; bulb planting for science. These activities can be meaningful at a number of levels, and we want all children to feel successful. In time, at their own individual paces, children will achieve the various goals of the alphabet program.

At our first parent meeting on _____ at _____ we will show you some of the activities in which your child is participating as part of the alphabet program. We know that you will enjoy watching your child achieve the goals of this program, and we look forward to working with both your child and you.

Sincerely,

A a

apple (See pattern, page 6.)

Apple Letter Project

Letter bag items*

abacus	animal
afghan	animal crackers
alligator	ant farm
alphabet	apple
ambulance	applesauce
anchor	

Multisensory letter projects

ambulance (See pattern and instructions, pages 4–5.)

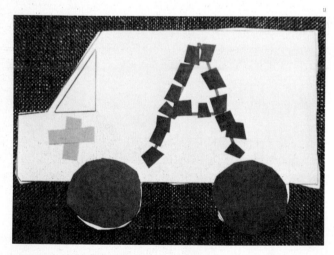

Ambulance Letter Project

*Items such as these are brought from home by the children. The first week is always a bit slow—both because vowels present special challenges and because children and parents are getting used to the program.

When vowels are introduced, the short sound is emphasized, but we discuss with the children that letters often have other sounds.

Other project

apple prints

■ Cut an apple horizontally so that the star shows. Have children dip the apple half in thick paint and print on construction paper.

Thinking skills

Comprehension:

■ Ask children to find specified objects on an apple bulletin board.

Find the animals on the apple bulletin board.

- Have children smell, look at, feel, taste and describe slices of different varieties of apples on an apple tasting tray.

- Have children compare parts of apples and whole apples.

- Show visual closure cards. (See examples, pages 7–12.)

Memory:

- Designate a "magic" page before reading a book. Have children quietly raise their hands if they recognize the page when it is reached in the story.

- Show three pictures of animals for one second each. Ask children to remember as many details as possible. Add to the number of pictures as children gain proficiency.

- Put items from the letter bag on a memory tray. Remove one and ask children what is missing.

Decision making:

- Have children classify a collection of wild and tame animals according to where they belong—in the zoo or on the farm.

- Have children classify different varieties of red, golden, and green apples. (There are many criteria that can be used: size, color, markings, etc.) Discuss the classifications.

Creativity:

- Have children brainstorm names of animals, especially those whose names begin with *a*. (The purpose of brainstorming is to give as many ideas as fluently as possible. Evaluation of whether the ideas fit the criterion can follow the brainstorming activity.)

Food projects

applesauce (*Cook and Learn*)
apple juice
apple salad (*Cook and Learn*)

Books

About Animals, by Richard Scarry. New York: Golden Press, 1976.

The Airplane Book, by Bob Ottum. Racine, Wis.: Golden Press, 1972.

Animal Babies, by Harry McNaught. New York: Random House, 1977.

Animal Fair, by Janet Stevens. New York: Holiday House, 1981.

The Animal Kids, by Lorinda Bryan Cavley. New York: Random House, 1977.

Ants, by Diana Ferguson, illustrated by Reginald Davis. New York: Wonder Books, 1977.

Apples: How They Grow, by Bruce McMillan. Boston: Houghton Mifflin, 1979.

Nobody Listens to Andrew, by Elizabeth Guilfoile, illustrated by Mary Stevens. New York: Scholastic Inc., 1957.

Who's Got the Apple? by Jan Loof (Translated and adapted by Ole Risom and Linda Hayward). New York: Random House, 1975.

Songs and fingerplays

The Apple Tree
Two little apples hanging from a tree
  (fists in air)
Two little apples looking at me
  (turn fists inward)
I shook the tree as hard as I could
  (shake fists)
Down came the apples
  (fists down)
My! They were good!
  (rub tummy)

–Author unknown–

The golden letter people prepare to lead the singing of the good bye song.

Apples
I opened an apple and what did I see?
A little green worm, looking at me!
Apples, apples, good to eat.
Apples hide a special treat.

–Author unknown–

Science projects

Sprout alfalfa seeds.
Study an ant farm.

Field trips and visitors

apple orchard
airport

Airport Field Trip

■ When children return from the field trip, have them dictate or write and illustrate experience stories about what they saw.

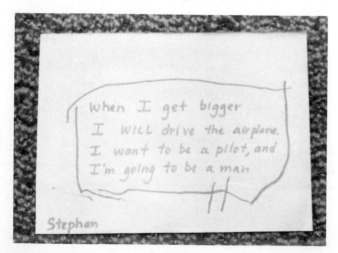

When I get bigger
I WILL drive the airplane.
I want to be a pilot, and
I'm going to be a man

Stephan

Airport Experience Story

ambulance driver

Instructions for Ambulance Letter Project

1. Precut or just draw the outline of the ambulance (depending on the age and capabilities of the children) on construction paper. Mark an upper-case *A* on the ambulance. Use white or yellow paper, depending on local ambulance colors.

2. Precut construction paper strips of varied colors one-half inch wide.

3. Invite children to snip the strips into squares or rectangles and paste the pieces on the *A* to cover it. (Note that this procedure provides a nonthreatening beginning step for children who have had limited experience with scissors.)

4. Have children trace the *A* with their fingers.

5. Say *"Ambulance, A"* as you write it on their papers.

NOTE: Follow similar instructions for other letter projects.

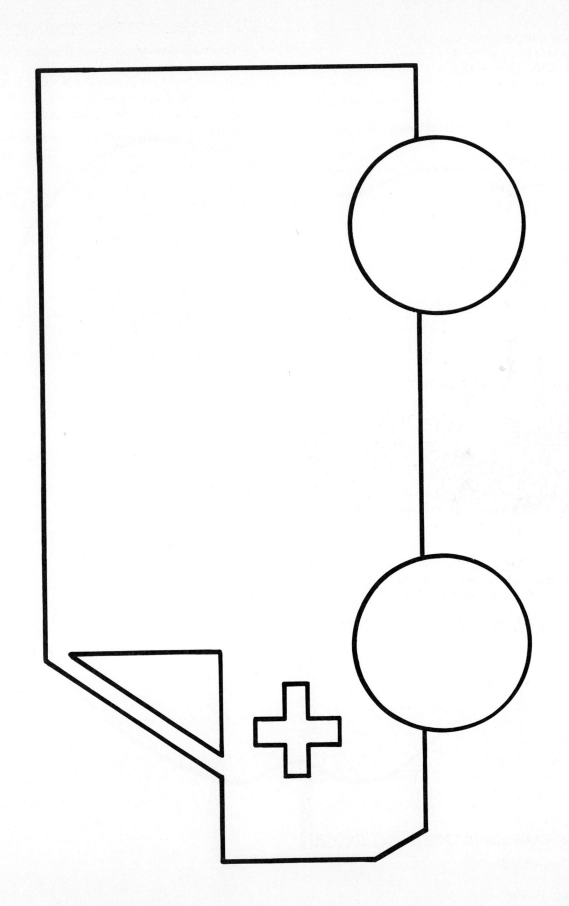

Multisensory letter project: ambulance   5

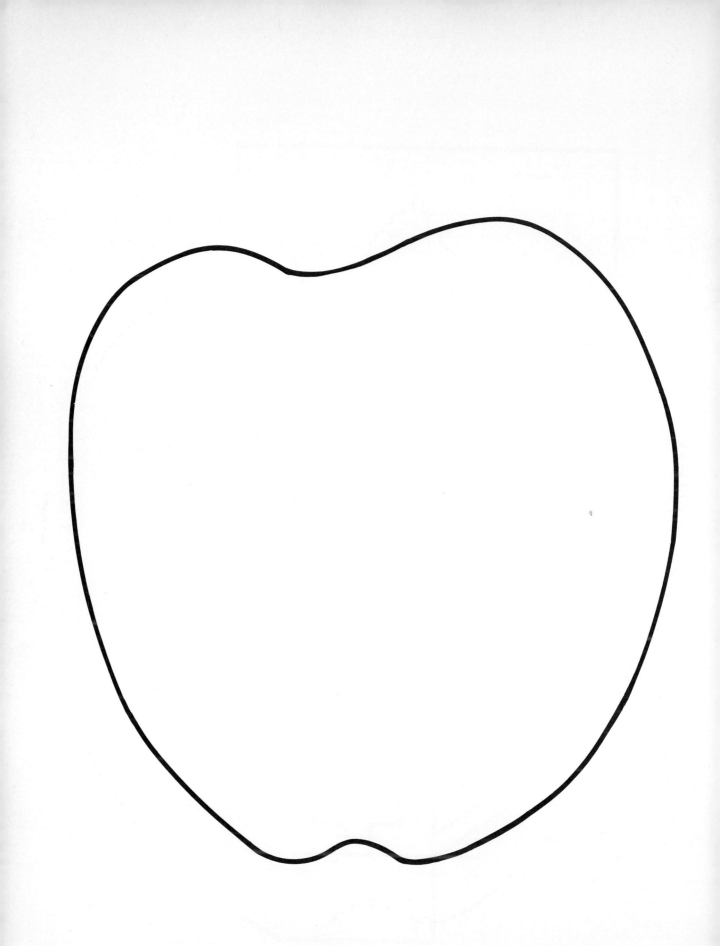

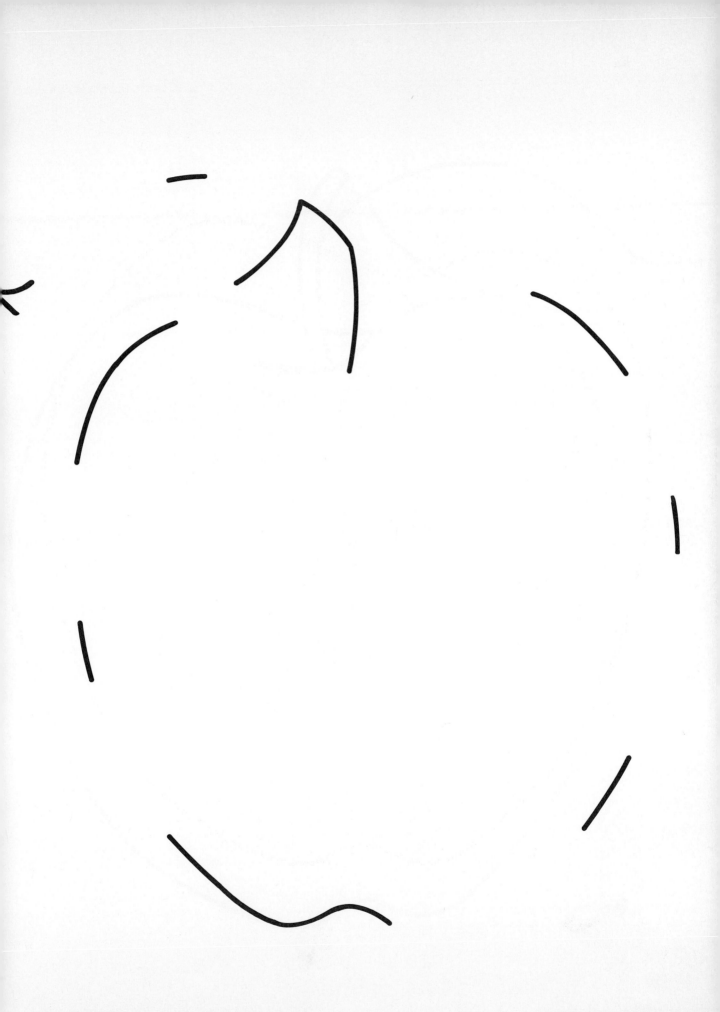

/Visual closure card: alligator

13

B b

Letter bag items

baby	beetle
balloon	bike
basket	bird
bat	butterfly
battery	boat
bean	bone
bear	bread
bee	button
berry	

Making Biscuits

Multisensory letter projects

bat (See pattern, page 17.)

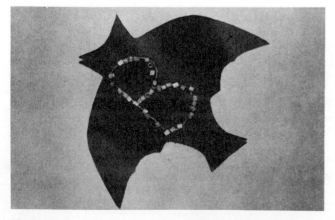

Bat Letter Project

bear (See pattern, page 18.)

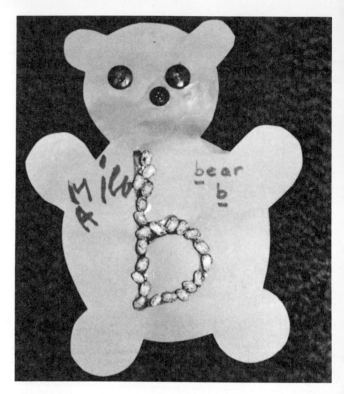

Bear Letter Project

Other projects

butterfly blotto (See pattern, page 19.)

■ Outline the butterfly on a large piece of construction paper. Have children apply paint to the wings on the right-hand side of the butterfly. Fold the butterfly in half at midline and rub gently. Open and observe the pattern on the wings.

bark rubbings

boat pictures

■ Have children make boats from popsicle sticks and paper shapes. Then have them dictate or write their ending to "If I had a boat . . .".

bubble painting

■ Mix tempera paint and liquid soap to a thin consistency. Pour into yogurt or cottage cheese containers. Provide a short length of straw for each child. Let children blow bubbles in containers so that bubbles froth and then have them lay a piece of paper lightly over the container. The bubble design will transfer.

bean collage

14

Barney Bear puppet (See pattern, page 20.)

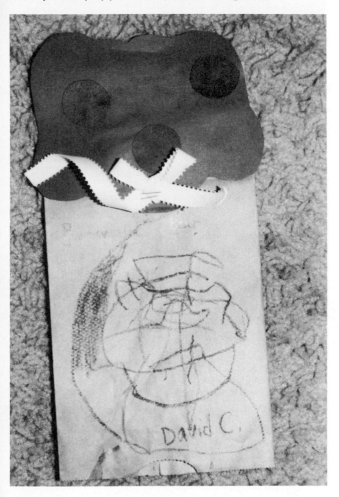

Barney Bear Puppet

Thinking skills

Comprehension:

- Have children duplicate bead patterns.

- Put out for exploration one of the following sets of objects: buttons, bows, brushes, baskets, balls, boxes, bags, or blocks. Have children touch, smell, feel, and describe items.

- Collect baby pictures of children. Discuss similarities, changes, growth, and development.

- Show visual closure cards. (See examples, pages 21–28.)

- Have children taste, smell, feel, look at, and describe various kinds of bread on a bread tasting tray.

Memory:

- Have children play *Concentration* using cards made from butterfly stickers. (To play, turn cards face down. Each player may turn two cards face up during each turn. If the cards match, the player keeps them. If they do not match, they are turned face down again.)

- Use the memory book with pictures of different birds.

- Designate "magic" pages in books that are read.

- Put items from the letter bag on the memory tray. Show the tray. Then cover it and ask the children to remember details about the items.

Decision making:

- Have children classify the items in one of the following groups: buttons, bows, brushes, baskets, balls, boxes, bags, or blocks. Discuss the classifications.

- Have children sort beans with tweezers.

Creativity:

- Have children brainstorm things to do with a blanket.

- Have children act out the story about the three bears.

- Have children choose magazine pictures of babies and dictate or write stories about them.

Food projects

biscuits (*Cook and Learn*)
bean salad (*Cook and Learn*)
beans
banana bread
butter (*Cook and Learn*)

Books

Ask Mr. Bear, by Marjorie Flack. New York: Macmillan, 1932.

Bears, by Ruth Krauss, illustrated by Phyllis Rowand. New York: Harper & Row, 1948.

The Bears Who Stayed Indoors, by Susanna Gretz. Chicago: Follett, 1971.

The Bear's Bicycle, by Emilie Warren McLeod, illustrated by David McPhail. Boston: Little, Brown and Company, 1975.

The Bear's Toothache, by David McPhail. Boston: Little, Brown and Company, 1972.

Benjamin's Book, by Alan Baker. New York: Lothrop, Lee, and Shepard, 1982.

Big Red Bus, by Ethel and Leonard Kessler. Garden City, New York: Doubleday, 1957.

Boat Book, by Gail Gibbons. New York: Holiday House, 1983.

Little Bear's Pancake Party, by Janice, illustrated by Mariana. New York: Lothrop, Lee, and Shepard, 1960.

Teddy Bears 1 to 10, by Susanna Gretz. Chicago: Follett, 1969.

Teddy Bears' Moving Day, by Susanna Gretz. New York: Four Winds Press, 1981.

The Winter Bear, by Ruth Craft and Erik Blegvad. New York: Atheneum, 1975.

Your Living Bones, by Louise G. McNamara and Ada B. Litchfield, illustrated by Pat G. Porter. Boston: Little, Brown and Company, 1973.

Songs and fingerplays

Row, Row, Row, Your Boat

Teddy Bear
Teddy bear, Teddy bear, turn around.
Teddy bear, Teddy bear, touch the ground.
Teddy bear, Teddy bear, show your shoe.
Teddy bear, Teddy bear, that will do.
Teddy bear, Teddy bear, go upstairs.
Teddy bear, Teddy bear, say your prayers.
Teddy bear, Teddy bear, turn out the light.
Teddy bear, Teddy bear, say good-night.
–Author unknown–

Bunny
Here comes a bunny
Hip-hop-hop
See how his long ears
Flip-flop-flop
See how his nose goes
Twink-twink-twink
See how his eyes go
Wink-wink-wink
Here is a bunny
With ears so funny

And here is his hole in the ground
A noise he hears
And he pricks up his ears
And he jumps in his hole in the ground.
–Author unknown–

Science projects

Plant bulbs.
Sprout beans.
Bake bread.

Field trips and visitors

bakery
barn
beauty/barber shops
butcher
baseball game
bee keeper

Additional ideas

bear day (See invitation, page 29.)

Special bears came to school for bear day.

Place on
fold

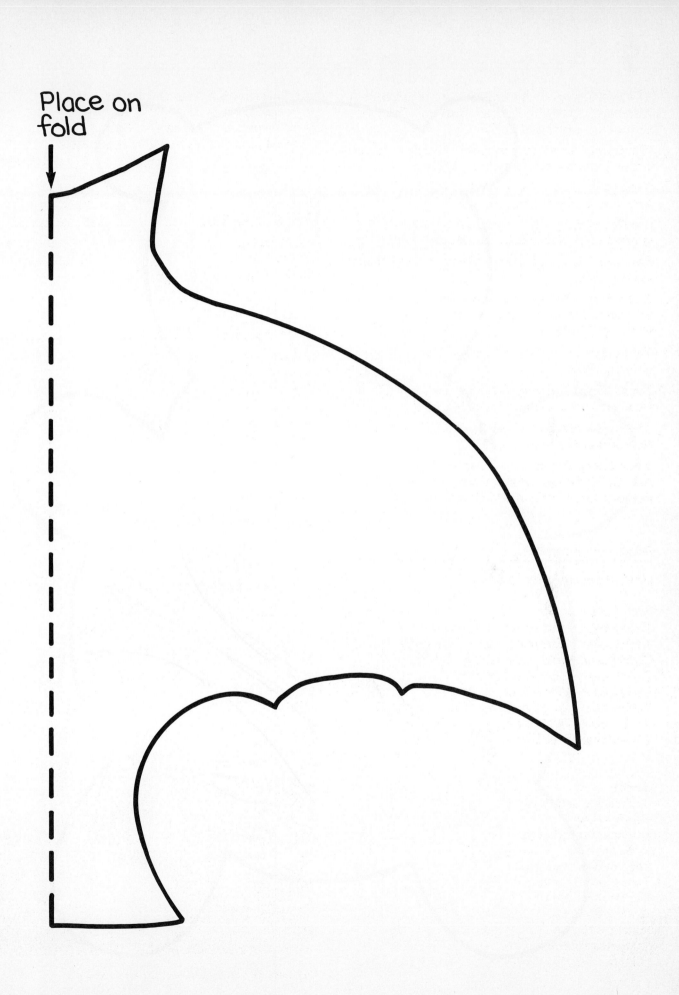

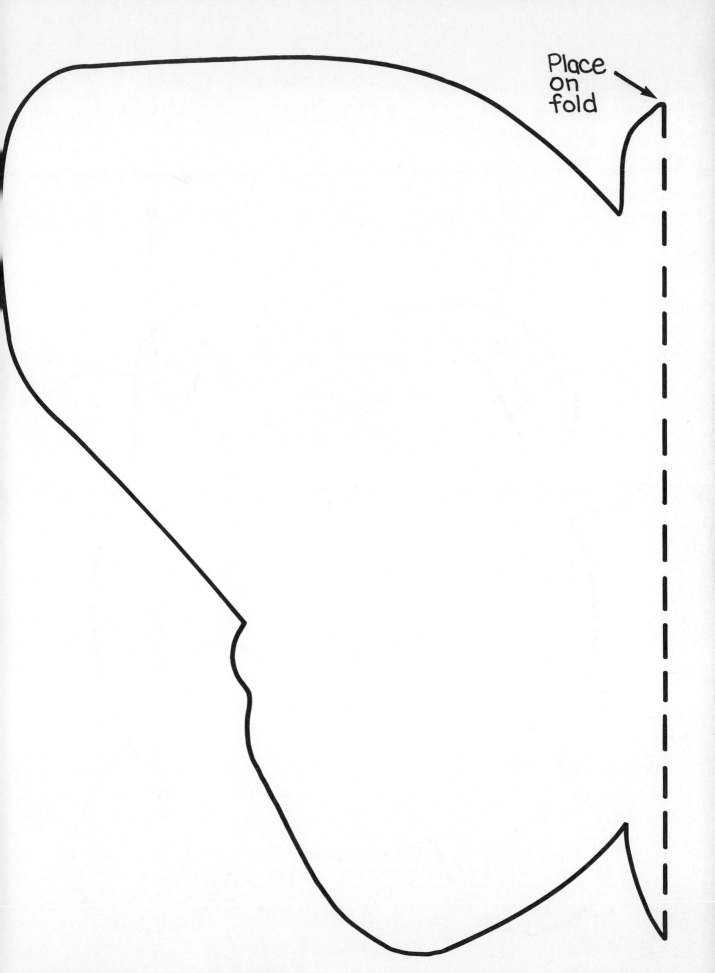

Place
on
fold

Butterfly blotto   19

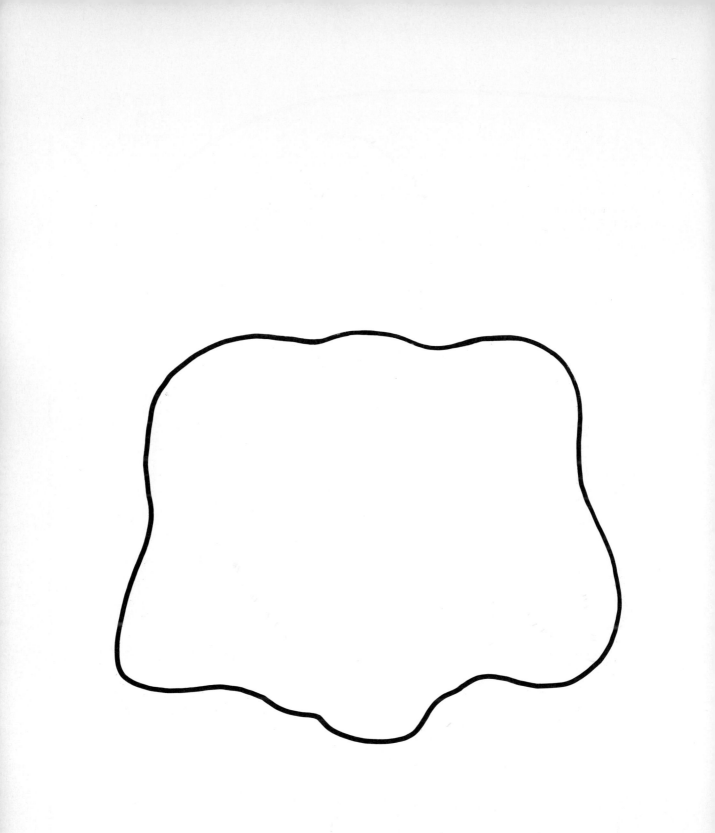

24 Visual closure card: banana

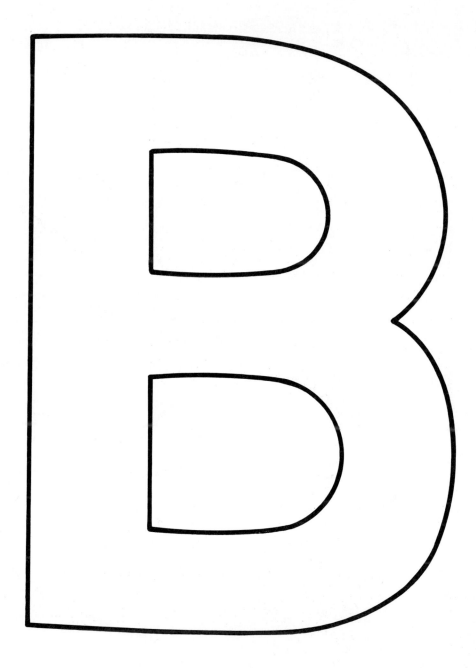

Visual closure card: *B*/Golden letter

On _____, children are invited to bring their special bear friends to school.

We will celebrate "Bear Day" with special songs, activities and a snack.

Please make sure that each "guest" is clearly labeled.

Thank you.

Cc

caboose (See pattern, pages 36–37.)

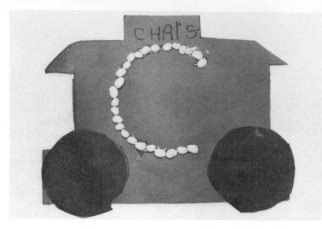

Caboose Letter Project

Letter bag items*

camel
camera
candle
car
carrot
cat
caterpiller

clock
clothespin
clown
comb
cork
crab

Multisensory letter projects

cat (See pattern, page 35.)

Cat Letter Project

*The hard *C* sound is emphasized, but we discuss with the children that letters often have other sounds.

Other projects

clown face (See pattern, pages 38–39.)

■ Ask children to arrange any combination of precut geometric shapes on a large white circle to make a clown face. Let children share their faces and any comments they have about their choices. Before they paste or glue, have children clear off all pieces, create another face, and tell about the new clown. Then ask children to paste or glue their favorite clown face.

Clown Face

cardboard collage

cookie cutter printing

crepe paper collage

- Show children how to paint liquid starch on construction paper and attach crepe paper while starch is wet.

cutting catalogs

car painting

- Have children dip small metal cars in paint and "drive" cars back and forth over a large sheet of paper.

Concentration cards

- Cut heavy paper into card-sized pieces. Help children select and attach pairs of stickers to make cards for playing *Concentration*. (See page 15 for playing directions.)

canoe lacing

- Cut a double canoe shape. (See pattern, page 40.) Punch holes all around the edges. Tie one end of the yarn to the canoe. Stiffen the other end of the yarn with a piece of tape. Have children put the yarn in and out of the holes.

Thinking skills

Comprehension:

- Present a corn exploration tray for children to taste, smell, look at, feel, and describe various forms of corn. Possible items are popcorn, corn nuts, canned corn, creamed corn, frozen corn, fresh corn on the cob.

- Have children move cars through a maze created on a table top.

- Show visual closure cards. (See examples, pages 41–50.)

Memory:

- Designate "magic" pages in books that are read.

- Play *Concentration* using the cards made as a craft activity.

- Use the memory book with pictures of *C* objects.

- Use the memory tray with items from the letter bag.

Decision making:

- Have children start collections of rocks, leaves, bottle caps, etc.

- Have children classify the items in one of the following groups: cars, corks, cans, cards, crayons. Discuss the classifications.

Creativity:

- Have children brainstorm colors or things found in cans or things that are cold.

Food projects

cole slaw (*Cook and Learn*)
cupcakes (*Cook and Learn*)
carrot salad (*Cook and Learn*)
corn fritters (*Cook and Learn*)

Books

Carousel, by Donald Crews. New York: Greenwillow Books, 1982.

Carrot Cake, by Nonny Hogrogian. New York: Greenwillow Books, 1977.

Clifford, the Small Red Puppy, by Norman Bridwell. New York: Scholastic Inc., 1972. (All of the other Clifford books would also be appropriate.)

Conrad's Castle, by Ben Shecter. New York: Harper & Row, 1967.

Corduroy, by Don Freeman. New York: Penguin Books, 1977.

Hi, Cat! by Ezra Jack Keats. New York: Macmillan, 1970.

Sally's Caterpillar, by Anne and Harlow Rockwell. New York: Parents Magazine Press, 1966.

There's a Nightmare in My Closet, by Mercer Mayer. New York: Dial Press, 1968.

The Toolbox, by Anne and Harlow Rockwell. New York: Macmillan, 1971. (This book introduces the tools of carpenters.)

The Very Hungry Caterpillar, by Eric Carle. New York: Scholastic Inc.

Songs and fingerplays

Caterpillar
Caterpillar, caterpillar,
Brown and furry,
    (Move cupped hand up arm.)
Winter is coming and
You'd better hurry!
    (Move hand faster.)
Find a big leaf,
Under which to creep
    (Mold one hand over other.)
Spin a cocoon in which to sleep.
    (Put hands beside face; close eyes.)
Then when spring time comes,
One fine day,
You'll be a butterfly,
And fly away!
    (Move arms as if flying.)

                    –Author unknown–

Carpenter
The carpenter's hammer goes tap, tap, tap.
    (Pound fists together.)
And his saw goes see, saw, see.
    (Saw left arm with right hand.)
And he planes and he measures.
    *(Bend fingers of one hand and move down
    other arm.)*
And he hammers and he saws,
    (Hammer and saw as before.)
While he builds a house for me.
    *(Form a house shape with arms bent
    at elbows.)*

                    –Author unknown–

This Little Clown
This little clown is fat and gay.
    (Hold up thumb.)
This little clown does tricks all day.
    (Hold up index finger.)
This little clown is tall and strong.
    (Hold up middle finger.)
This little clown is wee and small.
    (Hold up ring finger.)
And this little clown can do anything at all!
    (Hold up little finger.)

                    –Author unknown–

Science projects

Sprout carrot tops.
Study caterpillars.

Mix colors.

- Use white toothpaste as a base. Add food coloring in red, blue, yellow. Give each child the three primary colors and encourage them to mix new colors.

Field trips and visitors

country
cow pasture
camp (and set up a tent)
clown
computer center or shop

A clown came for a visit.

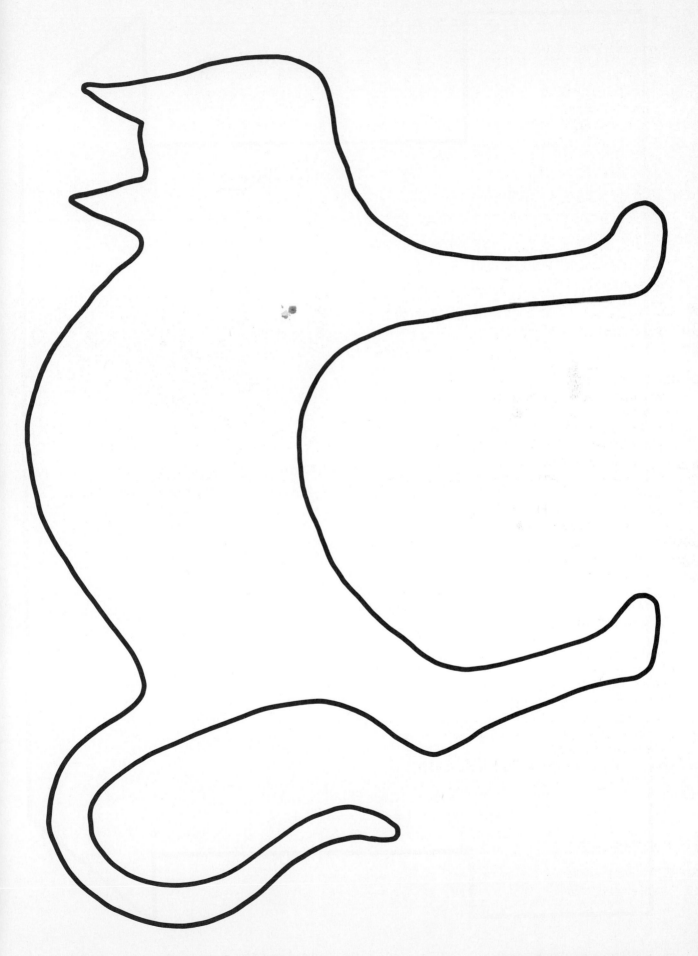

Multisensory letter project: cat 35

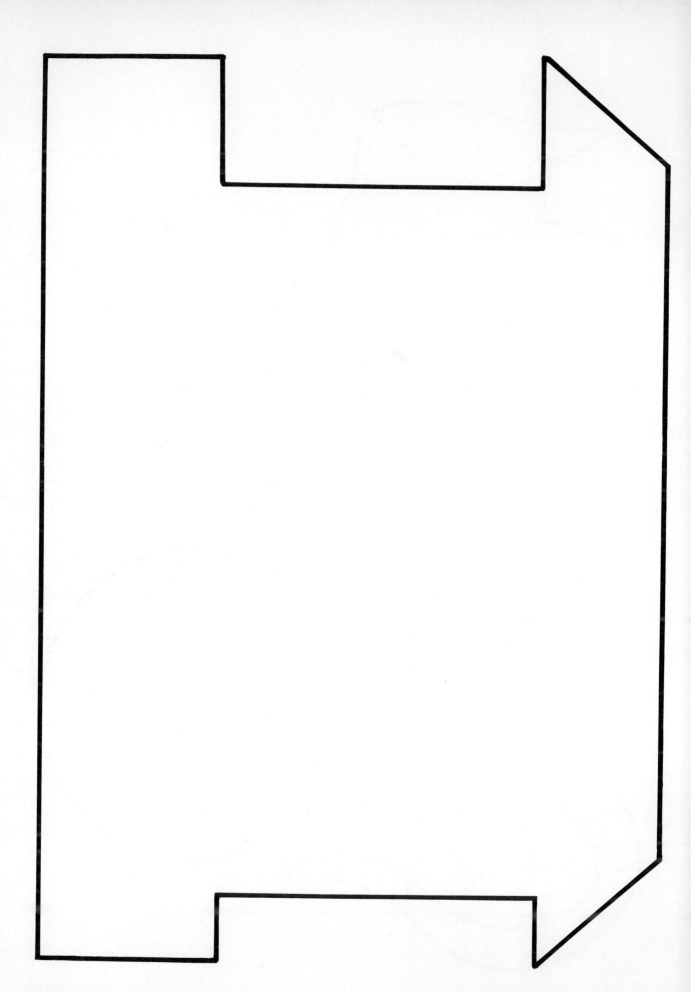

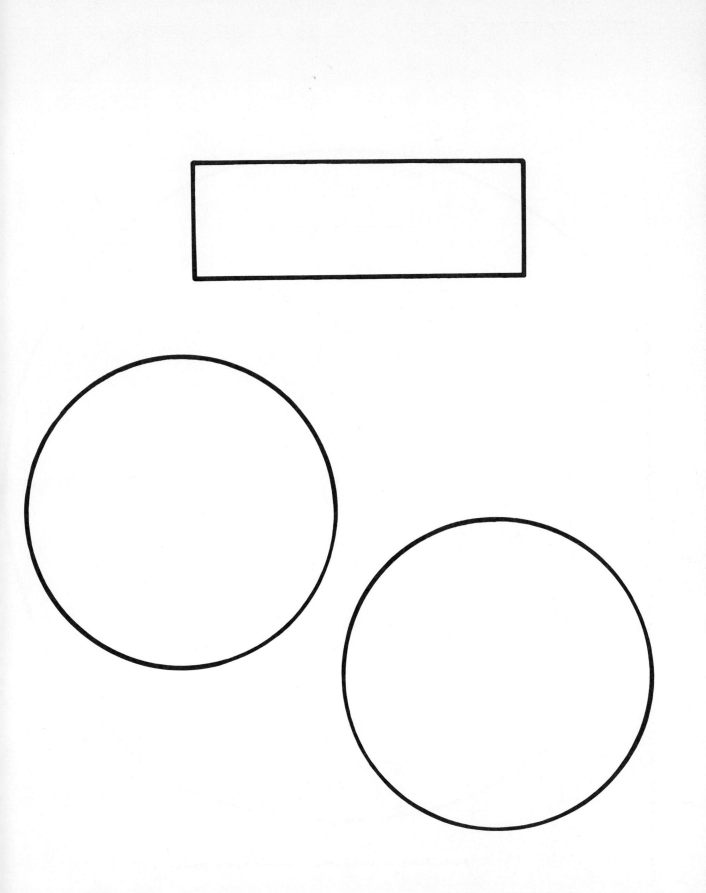

Multisensory letter project: caboose wheels and top   37

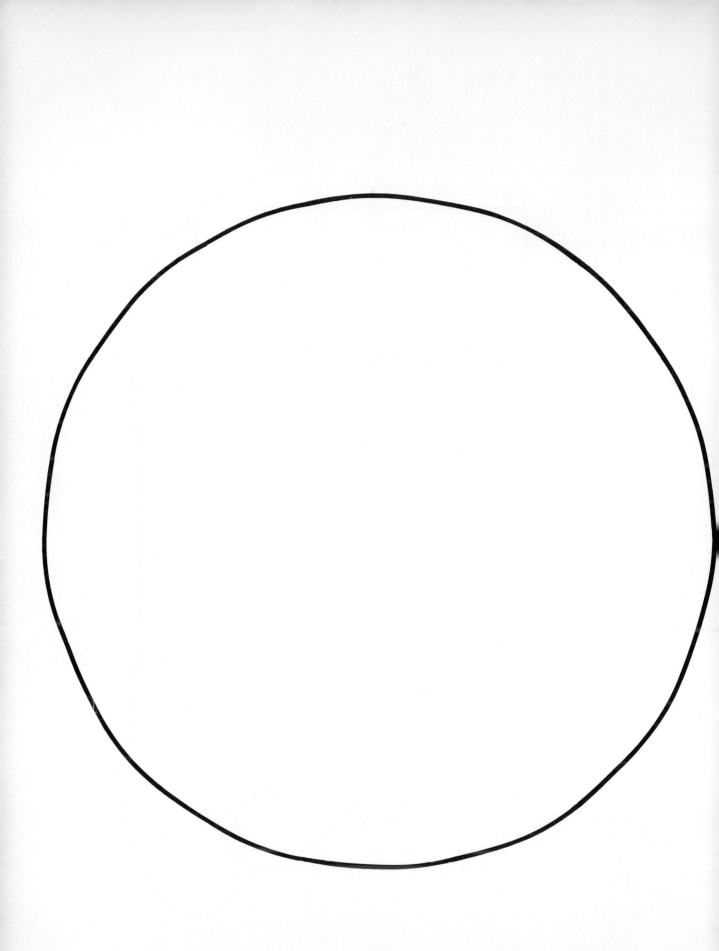

38　Clown project: face

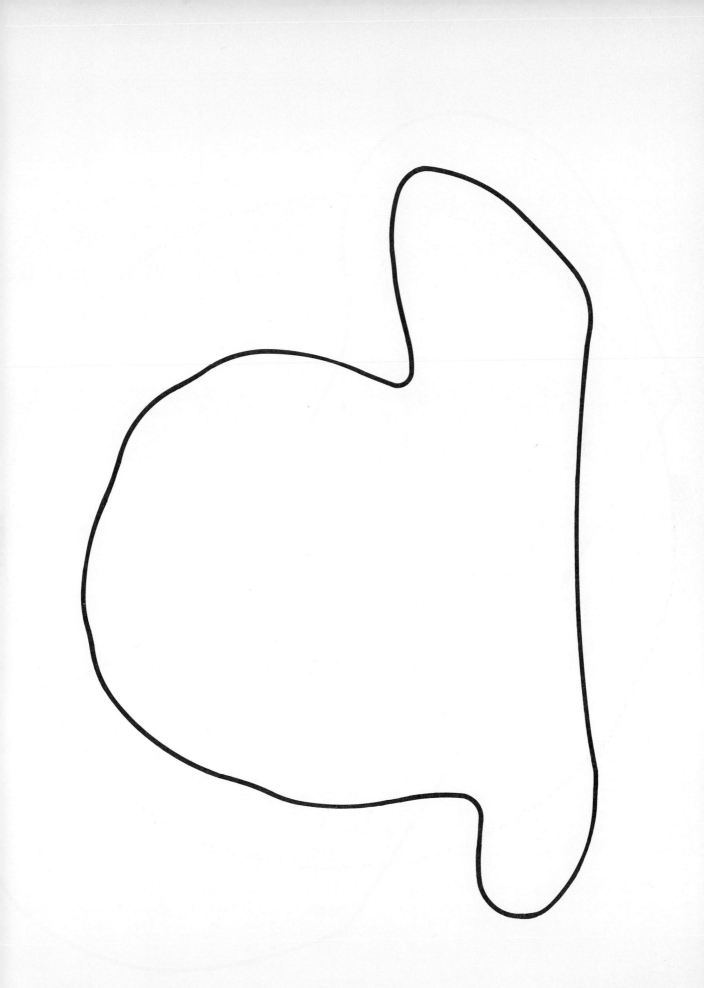

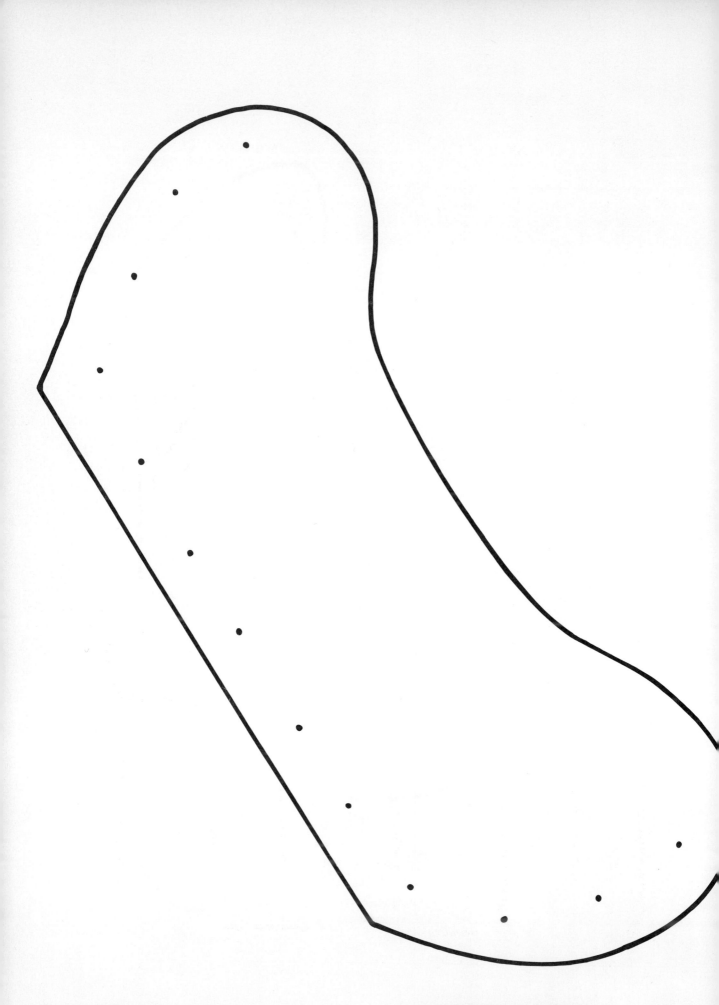

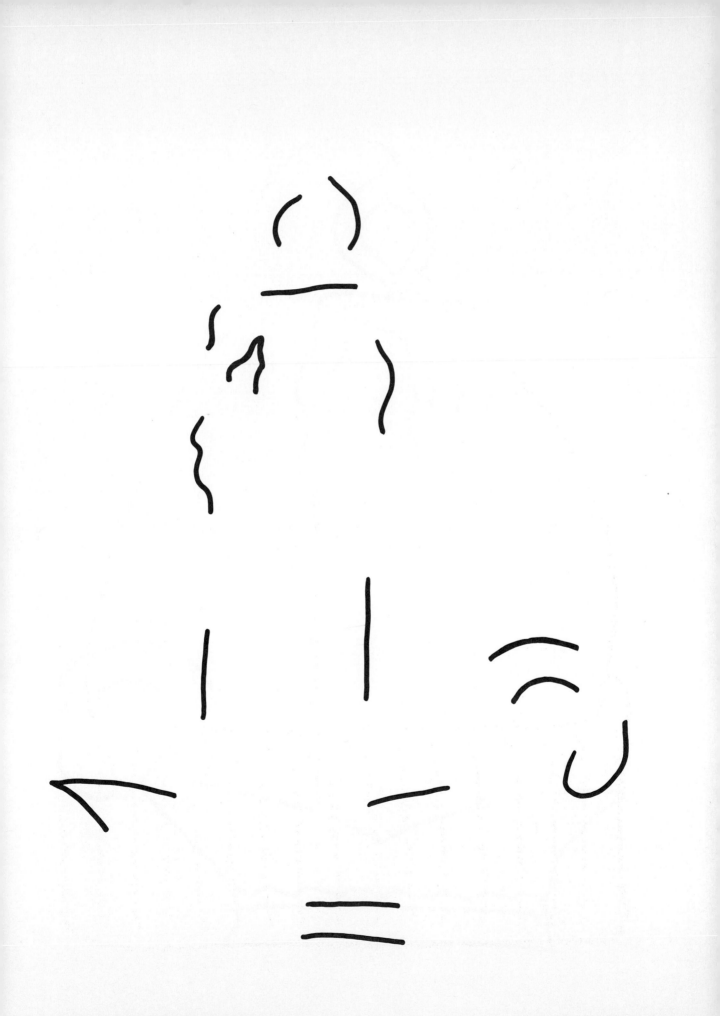

Visual closure card: candle

46   Visual closure card: camel

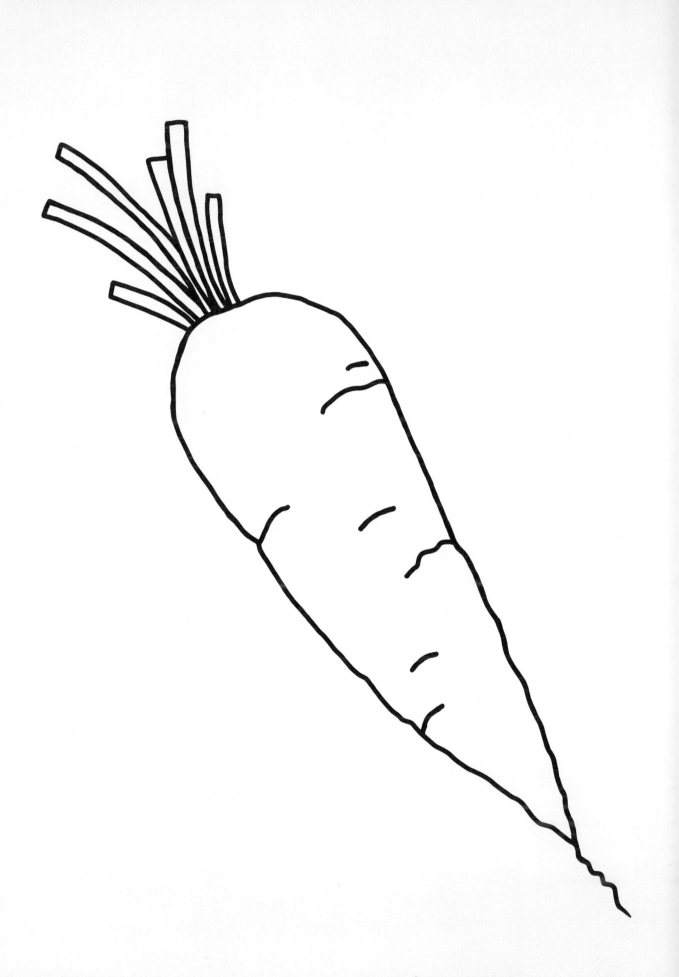

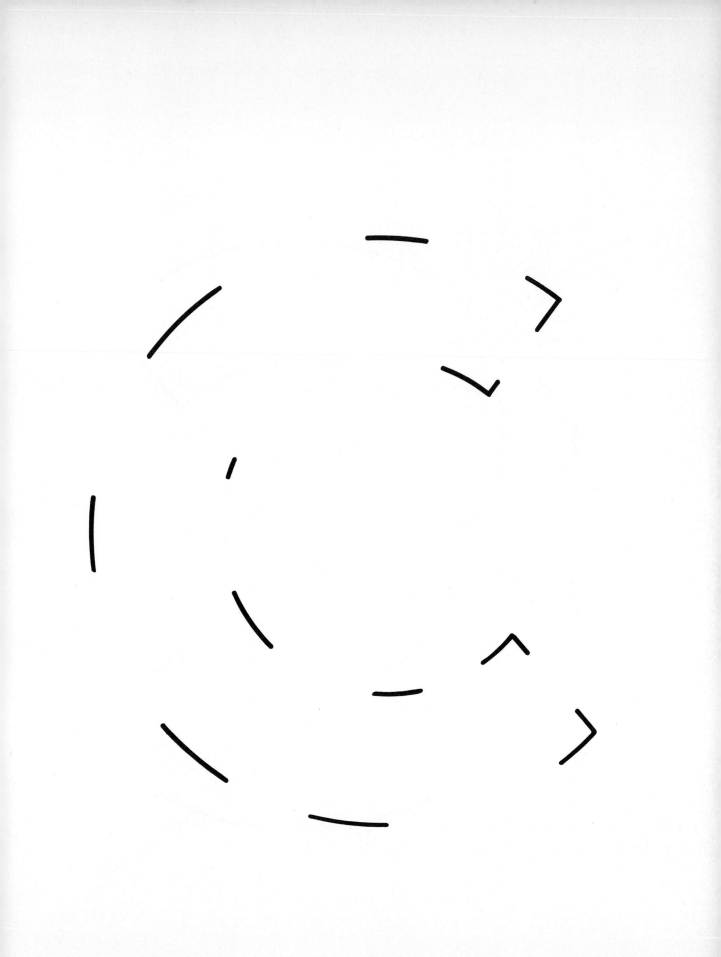

D d

Dd

Letter bag items

deer	doily
desk	doll
dice	dolphin
dime	domino
dinosaur	drum
dish	duck
dog	

Multisensory letter projects

daisy (See pattern, page 55.)

Daisy Letter Project

dog (See pattern, page 56.)

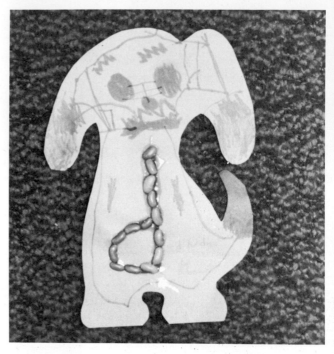

Dog Letter Project

Other projects

disguises (moustaches, hats, etc.)

drawing of life-size child

- On butcher paper, draw around each child. Then let children color their drawings.

magic door pictures

- Have each child decorate a "magic door" on construction paper. They then write or dictate stories about what could be behind the magic door.

Thinking skills

Comprehension:

- Have children dig holes in dirt. Identify deep, deeper, deepest.
- Use visual closure cards (See examples, pages 57–60.)
- Help children play dominoes.
- Have children explore one of the following sets of objects: dolls, dogs, drivers, drinks, dishes, or dinosaurs. Have children touch, smell, and describe items.

- Provide a tasting tray for children to smell, look at, feel, taste, and describe dairy products.

Memory:
- Use the memory tray with items from the letter bag.
- Let children play *Concentration* using cards made with dog stickers.
- Use the memory book with pictures of various dinner foods.
- Designate "magic" pages in books that are read.

Decision making:
- Have children classify the items in one of the following groups: dolls, dogs, drivers, drinks, dishes, or dinosaurs. Discuss the classifications.
- Ask children to find magazine pictures of dairy products.

Creativity:
- Have children brainstorm foods to eat for dinner.

Food projects

doughnuts
- Provide one tube-type refrigerator baking biscuit per child. Have children gently flatten the biscuits and push their fingers through the center to create a hole. Heat one inch of cooking oil in an electric frying pan to hot (375°). Place doughnut in oil and fry on both sides until golden brown. Remove doughnut from oil with tongs and have children shake in a brown paper bag with powdered sugar or cinnamon and sugar mixture.

dip for raw vegetables
date tasting

Books

Dance Away, by George Shannon, illustrated by Jose Aruego and Ariane Dewey. New York: Greenwillow Books, 1982.

David and Dog, by Shirley Hughes. Englewood Cliffs, N.J.: Prentice-Hall, 1978.

Deep in the Forest, by Brinton Turkle. New York: E. P. Dutton & Co., 1976.

The Digging-est Dog, by Al Perkins, illustrated by Eric Gurney. New York: Random House, 1967.

Dinosaur Bone, by Stan and Jan Berenstain. New York: Beginner Books, 1980.

Dinosaur Hunt, by George O. Whitaker with Joan Meyers. New York: Harcourt, Brace, & World, 1965.

The Dinosaur World, by Edwin H. Colbert, illustrated by George and Paul Geygan. New York: Stravon Educational Press, 1977.

Dinosaur Story, by Joanna Cole, illustrated by Mort Künstler. New York: Morrow, 1974.

Dinosaurs and Other Prehistoric Animals, by Darlene Geis, illustrated by R. F. Peterson. New York: Grosset & Dunlap, 1959.

Dinosaurs and Their World, by Lawrence Pringle. New York: Harcourt, Brace, and World, 1968.

A Dozen Dinosaurs, by Richard W. Armour, illustrated by Paul Galdone. New York: McGraw-Hill, 1967.

Harry, the Dirty Dog, by Gene Zion, illustrated by Margaret Bloy Graham. New York: Harper & Row, 1956.

How to Dig a Hole to the Other Side of the World, by Faith McNulty, illustrated by Marc Simont. New York: Harper & Row, 1979.

Make Way for Ducklings, by Robert McCloskey. New York: The Viking Press, 1941.

My Visit to the Dinosaurs, by Aliki. New York: Thomas Y. Crowell, 1969.

Songs and fingerplays

Six Little Ducks
Six little ducks that I once knew—
Fat ones, skinny ones, wet ones, too.
But the one little duck with the feather on his back—
He ruled the others with a quack, quack, quack.
–Author unknown–

Knock-Knock
Knock on door
 (Tap on head.)
Peek in
 (Put hands above eyes, as if looking.)
Lift up latch
 (Put finger under nose.)
Walk right in
 (Move fingers to mouth.)
Chin chopper, chin chopper, chin chopper, chin
 (Tap under chin while saying these words.)
–Author unknown–

Science project

Study dinosaurs

Field trips and visitors

dentist
doctor
dairy

The children tasted dairy products.

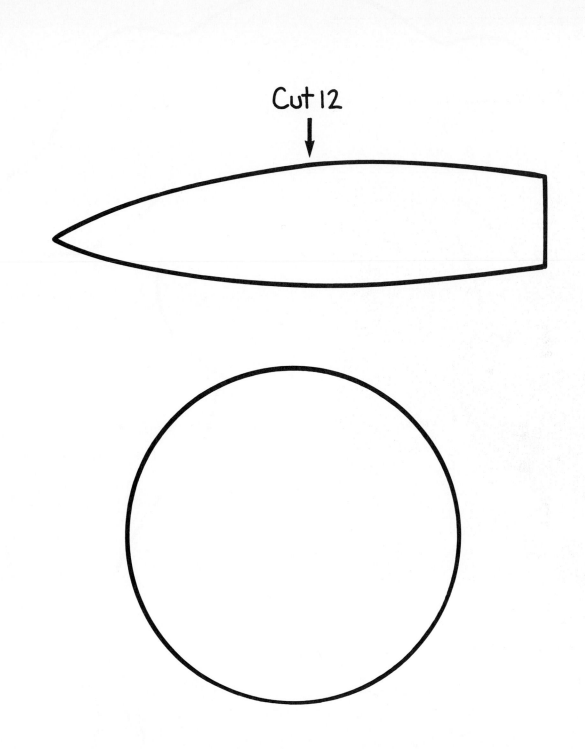

Cut 12

Multisensory letter project: dog

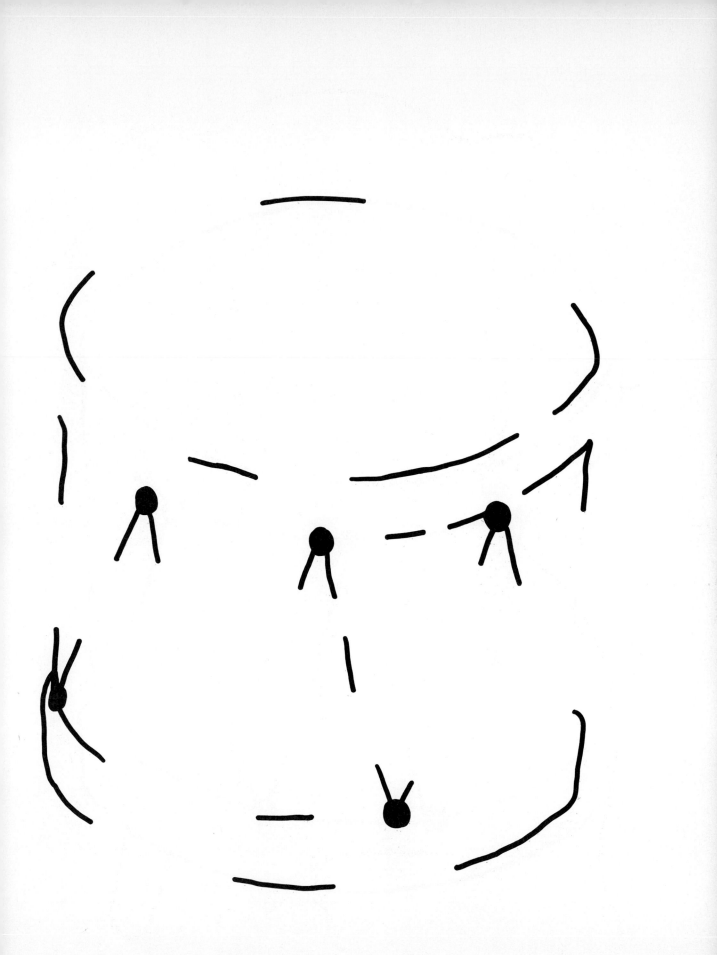

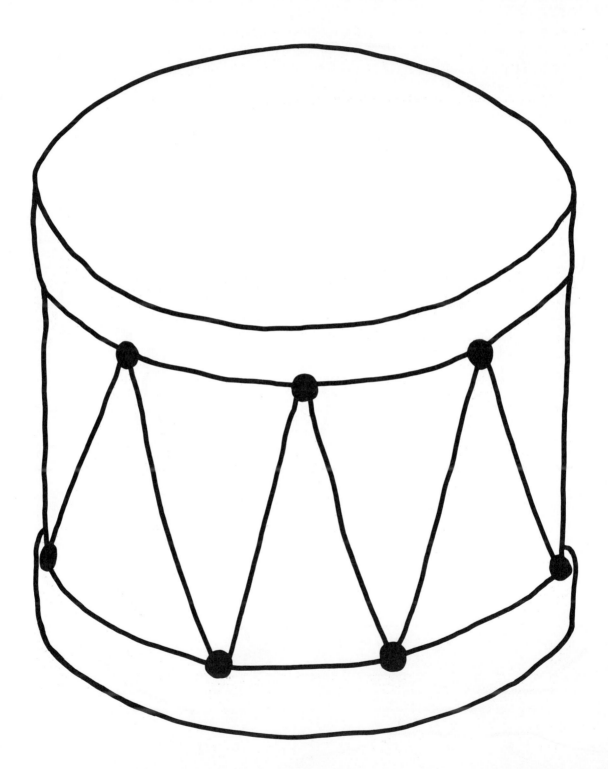

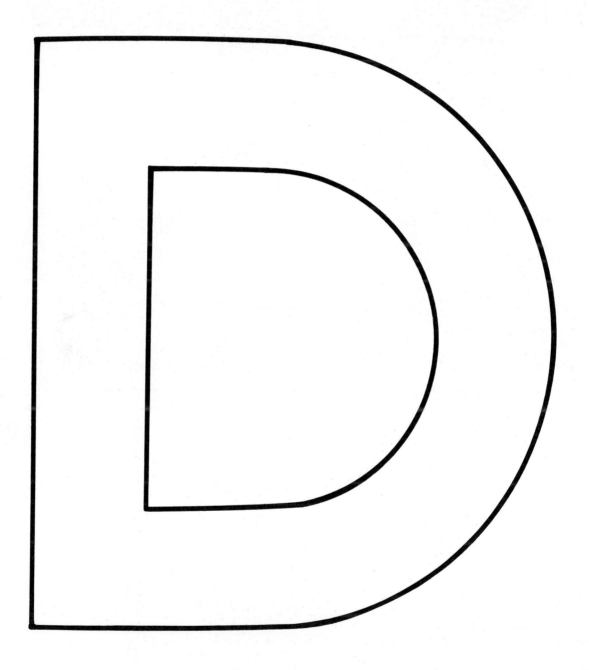

E

e

escalator

61

Ee

Letter bag items*

edge	elk
eggs	end
elastic	engine
elephant	envelope
elevator	escalator
eleven	Eskimo
elf	

Multisensory letter projects

elephant (See pattern, page 65.)

Elephant Letter Project

egg (See pattern, pages 66–67.)

Egg Letter Project

*When vowels are introduced, the short sound is emphasized, but we discuss with the children that letters often have other sounds.

Other projects

elephant ears (See pattern, page 68.)

- These are stapled on headbands for children to wear.

easel painting

Thinking skills

Comprehension:

- Explore the concepts of empty and full using items from the letter bag and a variety of containers.

- Use visual closure cards. (See examples, pages 69–72.)

- Have children explore one of the following sets of objects: eggs, elephants, erasers, or envelopes. Have children touch, smell, and describe items.

- Introduce election terminology and equipment: ballot, booth, ballot box, etc.

- Have children smell, look at, feel, and describe a broken egg.

Memory:

- Have children play a memory game with small *E* objects placed inside plastic eggs.

- Use the memory book with pictures of *E* objects.

- Designate "magic" pages in books that are read.

- Use the memory tray with items from the letter bag.

Decision making:

- Have children classify a set of plastic eggs by sound. (Fill the eggs in pairs with rice, pasta, paper clips, a bell, a marble, etc., and then glue them shut.)

- Have children classify the items in one of the following groups: eggs, elephants, erasers, or envelopes. Discuss the classifications.

- Take a vote by raised hands to elect the favorite *E* thing. The following day, use ballots to vote for a favorite color. Make a voting booth and a ballot box. On the ballots, color code with crayons the name of each color nominated. Count the votes and follow up by using the winning color at the easel, in play dough, and for construction paper on the following day.

Creativity:

- Have children write or dictate and illustrate a story about a place they would like to explore.

Food projects

eggs (*Cook and Learn*)
egg tasting (scrambled, soft boiled, hard boiled, poached, fried, raw)

Books

Clifford, the Small Red Puppy, by Norman Bridwell. New York: Scholastic Inc., 1972. (The main human character is Emily Elizabeth.)

Eggs, illustrated by Esme Eve. New York: Wonder Books, 1971.

Emily's Bunch, by Laura J. Numeroff and Alice N. Richter. New York: Macmillan, 1978.

Good Morning, Chick, by Mirra Ginsburg, illustrated by Byron Barton. New York: Greenwillow Books, 1980.

Let's Be Enemies, by Janice May Udry, illustrated by Maurice Sendak. New York: Harper & Row, 1961.

The Little Engine that Could, by Watty Piper, illustrated by George and Doris Hauman. New York: Scholastic Inc., 1961.

Uncle Elephant, by Arnold Lobel. New York: Scholastic Inc., 1981.

The World in the Candy Egg, by Alvin Tresselt, illustrated by Roger Duvoisin. New York: Lothrop, Lee, and Shepard, 1967.

Songs and fingerplays

The Elephant
The elephant has a trunk for a nose
  (Pretend an arm is the trunk.)
And up and down is the way it goes
  (Move arm up and down.)
He wears such a saggy, baggy hide
Do you think two elephants would fit inside?
  –Author unknown–

I am an Elephant
I am an elephant so big and strong,
I swing my trunk as I walk along
  (Rock back and forth, swing arm in front like trunk.)
I can walk fast, I can walk slow,
  (Walk fast and then slowly.)
And sometimes I like to stand just so.
  (Stand on one foot and lean to side.)
  –Author unknown–

Science project

Study evaporation.

- This can be done by marking water level in a clear jar, then observing and marking decreases.

Field trips and visitors

engine house
exploring (the neighborhood, a field, etc.)
election place
engineer

Children made imaginative engines.

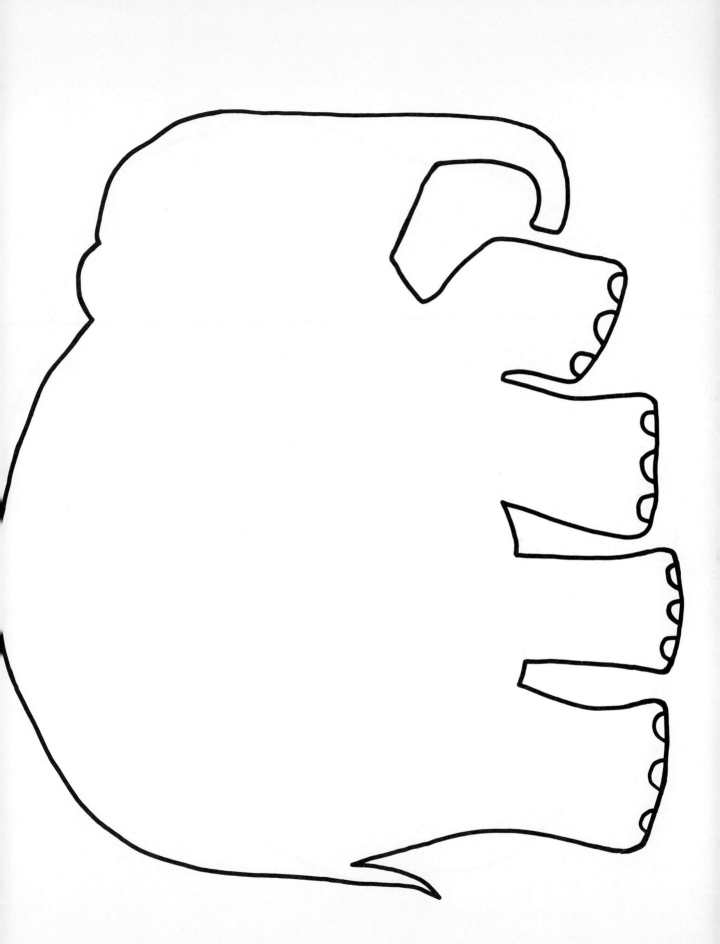

Multisensory letter project: elephant   65

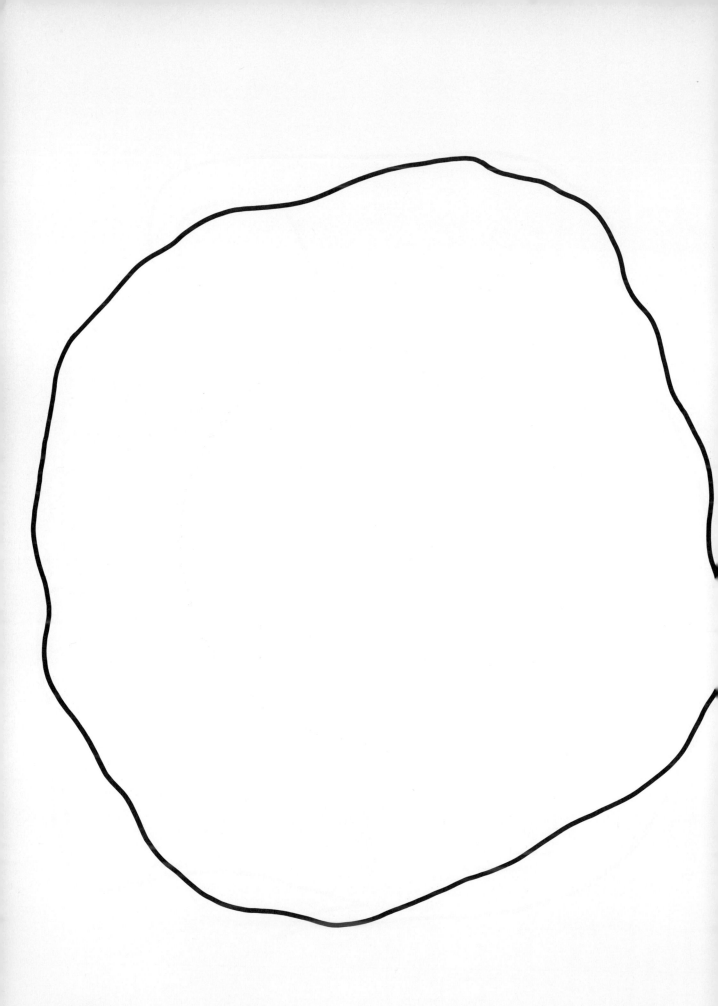

Multisensory letter project: egg white

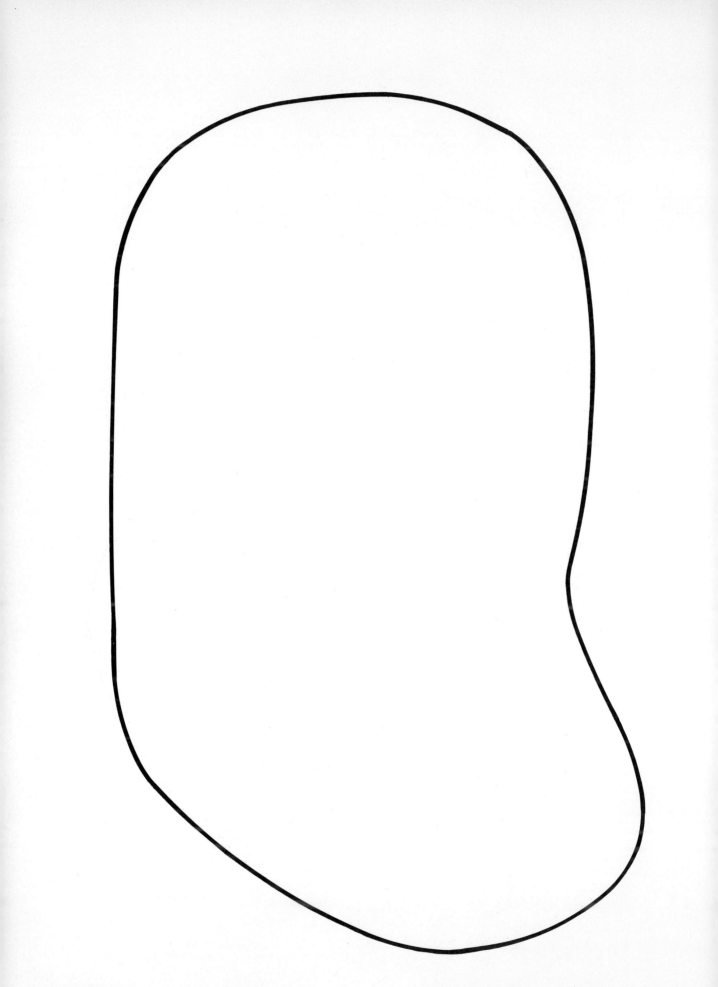

68   Elephant ear

70 Visual closure card: elephant

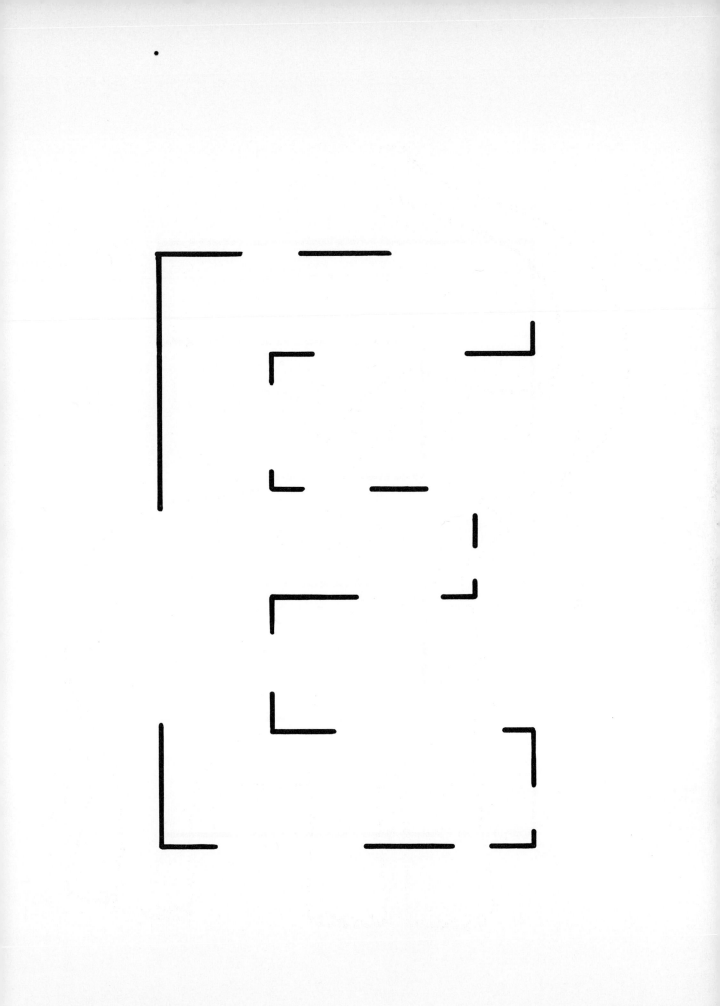

F f

73

F f

fox (See pattern, pages 78–79.)

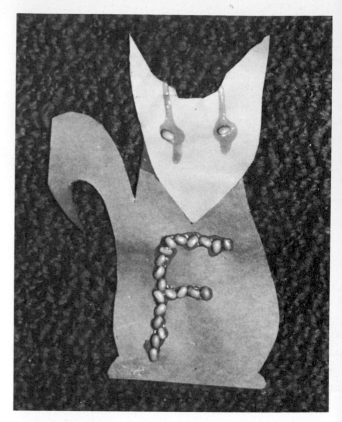

Fox Letter Project

Letter bag items

fan	flag
father	flower
feather	fork
fence	four
fig	fox
fire hat	frog
fish	fur
five	

Multisensory letter projects

frog (See pattern, page 77.)

Frog Letter Project

Other projects

fish collage

- Children choose a fish pattern from pages 80–82, add glue in the pattern of scales, then sprinkle confetti or glitter on the glue.

foot printing

- Have children sit down and make foot prints on butcher paper.

feather painting

- Have children use feathers instead of brushes to paint pictures.

family pictures

- Precut felt or construction paper into shirts, pants, and dresses. Make available circles and flat wooden sticks. Ask children to depict their families, using *their own* definitions, and to dictate or write a story.

Children depicted their families.

Thinking skills

Comprehension:

- Provide textured items for children to feel with their feet. (Four children can each be seated with their feet in a tub filled with rice, corn cobs, styrofoam, or fur pieces.) Have them describe the feeling and then rotate to another tub.

- Use visual closure cards. (See examples, pages 83–86.)

- Explore one of the following sets of objects: faces, fur, fabric, feathers, farm animals, flowers, or frogs. Have children touch, smell, and describe items.

- Discuss feelings: happy, sad, angry, scared, surprised, etc.

Memory:

- Use the memory tray with items from the letter bag.

- Use the memory book with pictures of various fish, flags, or farm animals.

- Let children play *Concentration* using cards made with farm animal stickers.

- Designate "magic" pages in books that are read.

Decision making:

- Have children classify the items in one of the following groups: faces, fish, flags, fur, fabric, feathers, farm animals, flowers, or frogs. Discuss the classifications.

Creativity:

- Have children brainstorm types of farm animals.

Food projects

fritter (*Cook and Learn*)
fruit salad (*Cook and Learn*)
French fries
fig tasting
fruit shake (*Cook and Learn*)

Books

A Birthday for Frances, by Russell Hoban, illustrated by Lillian Hoban. New York: Scholastic Inc., 1968.

Flip, by Wesley Dennis. New York: Scholastic Inc., 1973.

Flocks of Birds, by Charlotte Zolotow, illustrated by Ruth L. Bornstein. New York: Thomas Y. Crowell, 1965.

Fog in the Meadow, by Joanne Ryder, illustrated by Gail Owens. New York: Harper & Row, 1979.

The Foolish Frog, by Pete Seeger and Charles Seeger, illustrated by Miloslaw Jagr. New York: Macmillan, 1973.

Frederick, by Leo Lionni. New York: Pantheon, 1967.

The Frog Prince, by Paul Galdone. New York: McGraw-Hill, 1975.

Sometimes It's Turkey—Sometimes It's Feathers, by Lorna Balian. Nashville: Abingdon, 1973.

The Story of Ferdinand, by Munro Leaf, illustrated by Robert Lawson. New York: The Viking Press, 1936.

Songs and fingerplays

The More We Get Together
The more we get together
The happier we'll be
The more we get together
The happier we'll be
For your friends are my friends
And my friends are your friends
The more we get together
The happier we'll be.

–Author unknown–

Put Your Finger in the Air
Put your finger in the air, in the air.
Put your finger in the air, in the air.
Put your finger in the air and leave it right up there.
Put your finger in the air, in the air.

–Author unknown–

Ten Little Fingers
I have ten little fingers and they all belong to me.
  (Place hands upright.)
I can make them do things. Would you like to see?
I can shut them up tight.
  (Form fist.)
Or open them wide.
  (Open hands.)
I can put them together, or make them all hide.
  (Close both fists.)
I can make them jump high.
  (Put hands over head.)
I can make them go low.
  (Put hands down.)
I can fold them quietly and hold them just so.
  (Put hands in lap.)

–Author unknown–

Field trips and visitors

fire station
firefighter
farm

Fire Station Field Trip

Science projects

Freeze water.

Dissect fish.

■ The presentation in *World Book Encyclopedia* (Chicago: World Book, Inc., 1984, pp. 148h–148i) is an excellent reference. The teacher dissects the fish and points out the parts as children watch and refer to the book.

Identify objects that float.

Multisensory letter project: frog   77

Multisensory letter project: fox (body)   79

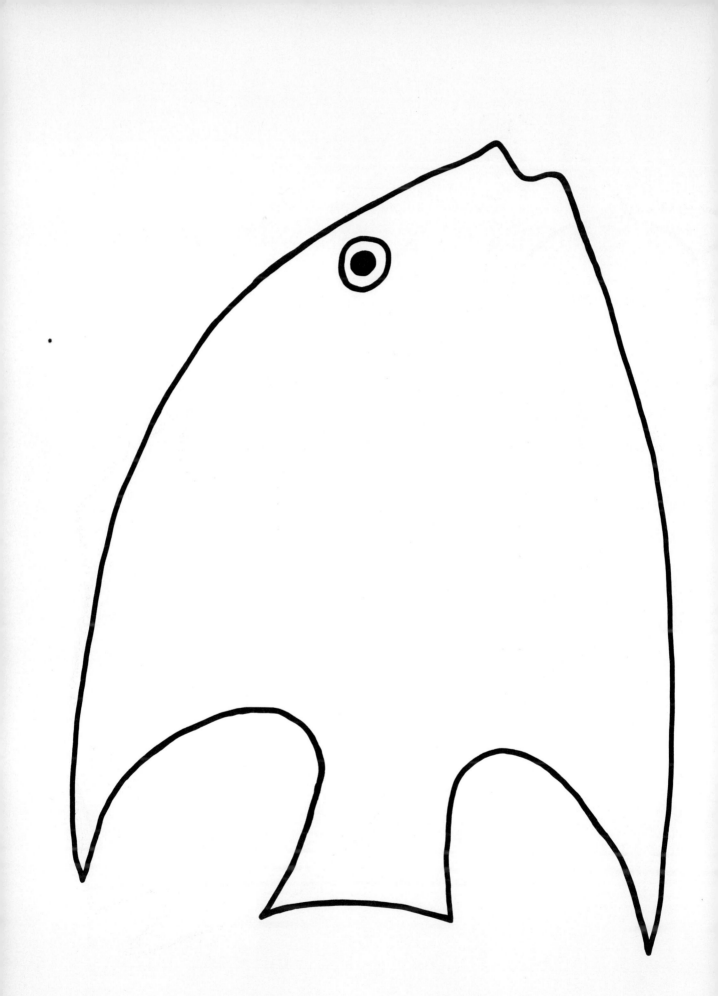

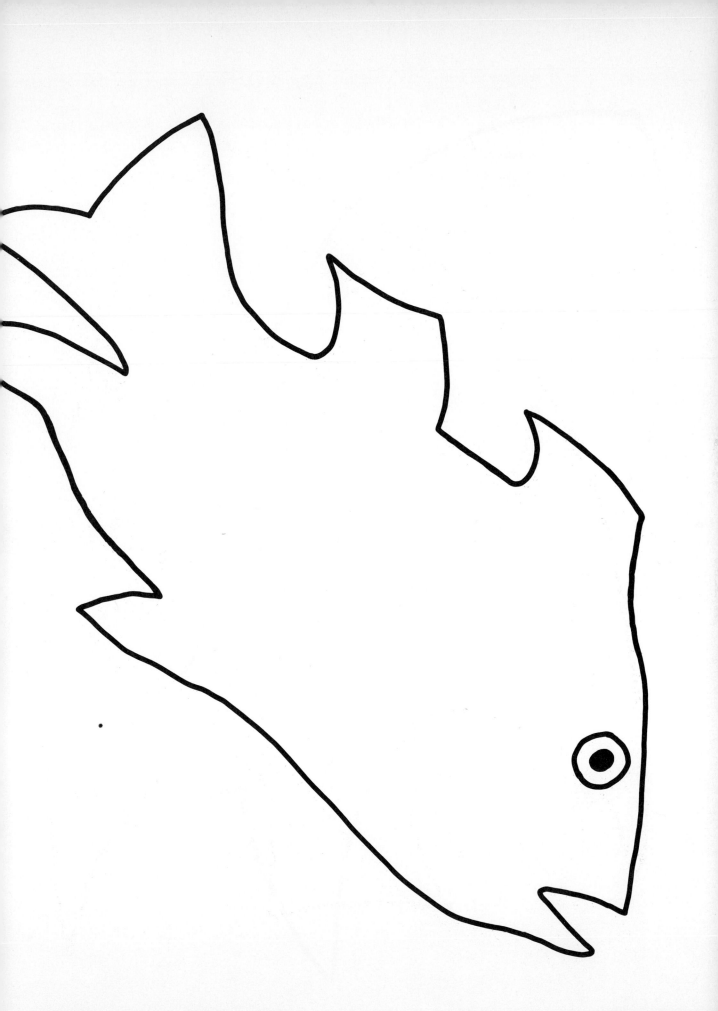

Fish collage   81

82 Fish collage

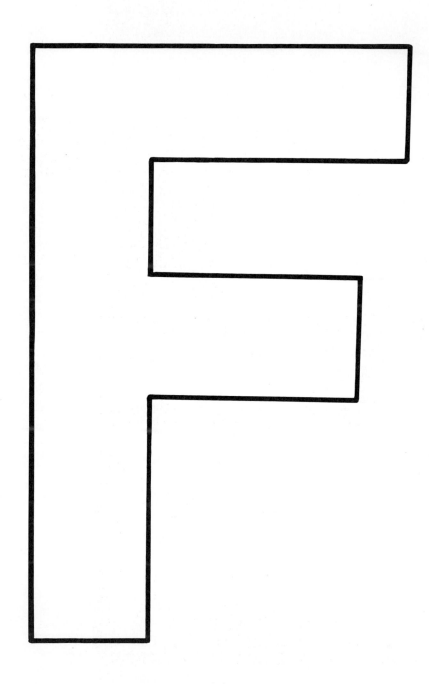

Visual closure card: *F*/Golden letter

G

G g

Letter bag items*

game	goat
garbage	goldfish
ghost	golf ball
gift	goose
girl	gourd
glass	grass
glasses	green
gloves	

Multisensory letter projects

goat (See pattern, page 91.)

Goat Letter Project

*The hard *G* sound is emphasized, but we discuss with the children that letters often have other sounds.

guitar (See pattern, page 92.)

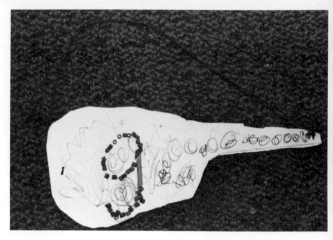

Guitar Letter Project

Other projects

creative writing experience: gift wish

- Fold a large sheet of paper in half. Have children select a bow for the front and then open to dictate or write about what they would like to give (and to whom).

green collage

garbage walk and collage

- Have children take sacks on a walk to collect litter and use it to make a class collage on butcher paper cut in the shape of a large garbage can.

green vegetable prints

Thinking skills

Comprehension:

- Have children taste, smell, look at, feel, and describe green vegetables on a tasting tray. Use green beans, lettuce, broccoli, green pepper, cabbage. Discuss differences between whole vegetables and parts.

- Use visual closure cards. (See examples, pages 93–96.)

- Provide a variety of gloves for children to explore: leather, rubber, cloth, yarn, garden, etc. Then have them try to recognize each type by touch alone.

- Play stop and go.

Memory:
- Use the memory tray with items from the letter bag.
- Use the memory book with pictures of *G* objects.
- Designate "magic" pages in books that are read.

Decision making:
- Have children classify a collection of gloves. Discuss the classifications.
- Ask children to classify green foods. Discuss the classifications.

Creativity:
- Have children brainstorm green things, things that grow, or things that can be gobbled.
- Let children act out the story of the *Three Billy Goats Gruff.*

Food projects

granola (*Cook and Learn*)
grilled cheese
green vegetable salad
gingerbread people (*Cook and Learn*)

Books

George and Martha, by James Marshall. New York: Scholastic Inc., 1972.

The Gingerbread Man, by Ed Arno. New York: Scholastic Inc., 1967.

Goggles, by Ezra Jack Keats. New York: Holt, Rinehart, and Winston, 1969.

Goosey Goosey Gander, illustrated by Stephen Weatherill. New York: Greenwillow Books, 1982.

My Grandson Lew, by Charlotte Zolotow, illustrated by William Pène DuBois. New York: Harper & Row, 1974.

Green Eggs and Ham, by Dr. Seuss. New York: Beginner Books, 1960.

The Grouchy Ladybug, by Eric Carle. New York: Thomas Y. Crowell, 1977.

In Granny's Garden, by Sarah Harrison & Mike Wilks. New York: Holt, Rinehart, and Winston, 1980.

The Three Billy Goats Gruff, by Susan Blair. New York: Scholastic Inc., 1967.

Songs and fingerplays

Growing, by Hap Palmer (*Learning Basic Skills Through Music* record, Educational Activities, Inc., Freeport, N.Y.)

Gobble, Gobble, Gobble
He's big and fat and gobble, gobble, gobble.
He spreads his tail and gobble, gobble, gobble.
But when Thanksgiving day is here
Then it's our turn to gobble, gobble, gobble.
        –Author unknown–

Science projects

Plant a garden.
Use magnifying glasses.
Observe and care for guinea pigs or gerbils.
Find out what happens to garbage in the community.
Sprout grass.

Field trips and visitors

garden
grocery store
gardener

A child drew his favorite *G* things.

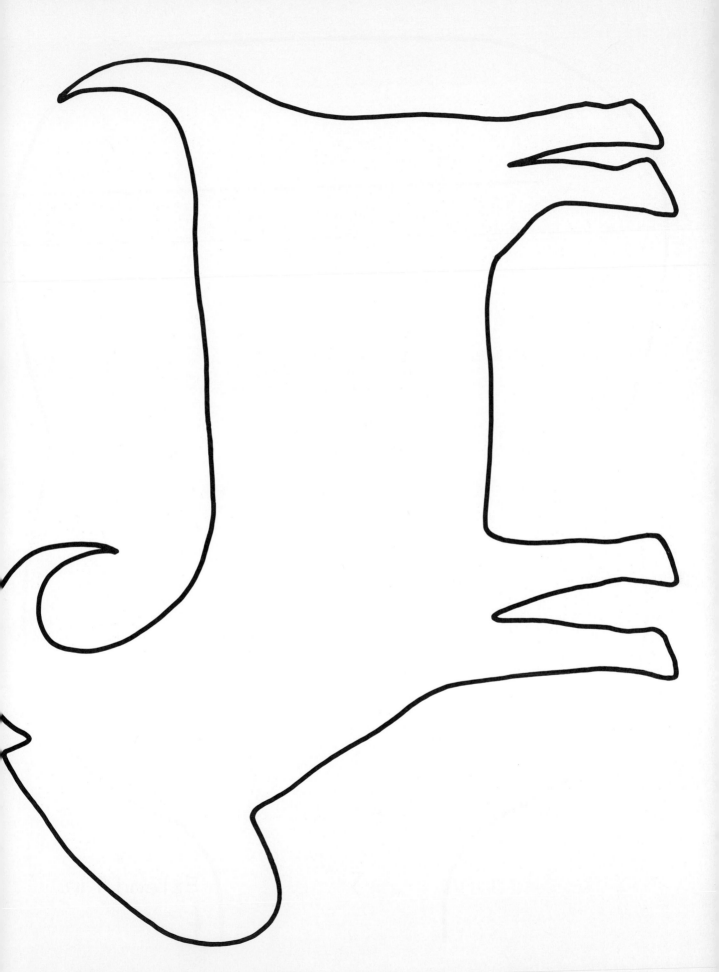

Multisensory letter project: goat   91

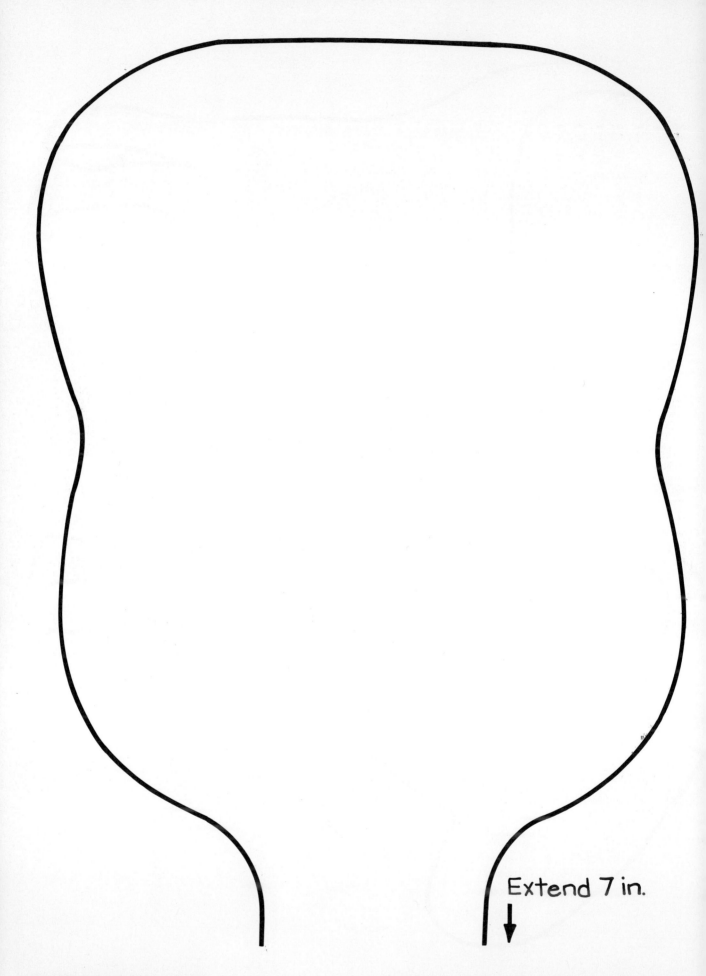

Extend 7 in.

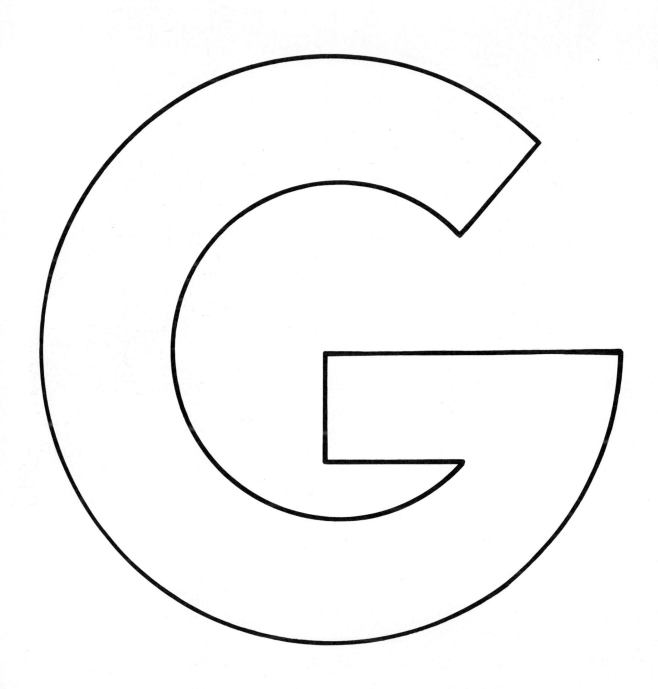

Visual closure card: *G*/Golden letter

H h

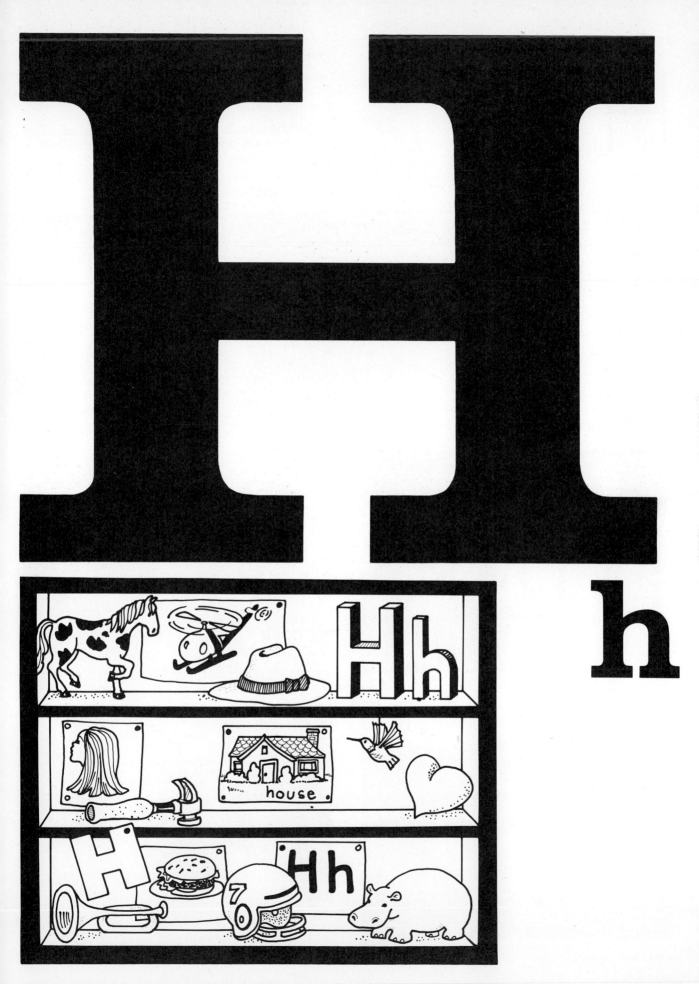

house

H h

Letter bag items

hammer	helicopter
hamster	helmet
hand	hen
handkerchief	hoe
harp	holly
hat	horn
hay	horse
head	

Multisensory letter projects

horse (See pattern, pages 101–102.)

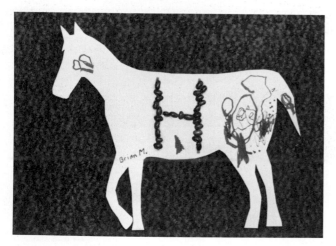

Horse Letter Project

hat (See pattern, page 103.)

Hat Letter project

Other projects

haunted house

- Cover milk cartons with black paper. Have children decorate them and then dictate or write scary stories.

hand prints

A child came up with his own idea for handprints.

headbands

Children made headbands with geometric shapes. This pattern used squares and hexagons.

98

houses from graham crackers

drawings (or collages of magazine pictures) of *things in my house*

home mural

- Have children draw their residences, including addresses. Mount the pictures on a mural showing a street.

Thinking skills

Comprehension:

- Have children explore the concepts of heavy and light using items from the letter bag and a simple balance scale.
- Have children study different types of homes.
- Ask children to listen (hear) and try to identify familiar noises by the sound alone.
- Introduce different community helpers, through pictures or in person.
- Have children explore one of the following sets of objects: hats, model horses, hearts, or things that belong in a house. Ask them to touch, smell, and describe the items.
- Use visual closure cards. (See examples, pages 104–107.)
- Have children examine and describe hair color, texture, length, etc.

Memory:

- Use the memory tray with small hats. (These can be obtained from craft stores that carry items for making dolls.)
- Use the memory book with pictures of *H* objects.
- Designate "magic" pages in books that are read.

Decision making:

- Have children classify the items in one of the following groups: hats, model horses, hearts, or things that belong in a house. Discuss the classifications.
- Have children match symbols with the appropriate holidays.

Creativity:

- Have children brainstorm things that can be heard; things to do to help; things that are hot, heavy, or hard.

- Let children act out the story of *The Little Red Hen.*
- Let children act out *Humpty Dumpty.*

Food projects

hamburgers
hush puppies (*Cook and Learn*)

Books

All the Pretty Horses, by Susan Jeffers. New York: Macmillan, 1974.

Harry by the Sea, by Gene Zion, illustrated by Margaret Bloy Graham. New York: Harper & Row, 1965.

Harry the Dirty Dog, by Gene Zion, illustrated by Margaret Bloy Graham. New York: Harper & Row, 1956.

How, Hippo! by Marcia Brown. New York: Charles Scribner's Sons, 1969.

Humpty Dumpty, illustrated by Stephen Weatherill. New York: Greenwillow Books, 1982.

It Hardly Seems Like Halloween, by David S. Rose. New York: Lothrop, Lee and Shepard, 1983.

The Little House, by Virginia Lee Burton. Boston: Houghton Mifflin, 1969.

The Little Red Hen, by Paul Galdone. New York: Scholastic Inc., 1973.

My Hands, by Aliki. New York: Thomas Y. Crowell, 1962.

Who Took the Farmer's Hat? by Joan L. Nodset, illustrated by Fritz Siebel. New York: Harper & Row, 1963.

Songs and fingerplays

Homes
Here is a house for a robin
  (Open hand.)
Here is a hive for a bee.
  (Close hand.)
Here is a hole for a bunny.
  (Make a circle with fingers.)
Here is a home for me.
  (Gesture around.)

  –Author unknown–

If You're Happy and You Know It . . .
Head, Shoulders, Knees, and Toes
Humpty Dumpty

Science projects

Study animal homes, habitats, hibernation.
Study the heart.
Study health.
Look at hair under a microscope.

Field trips and visitors

hairdresser
hardware store
hospital

Additional ideas

Share hobbies.
Hop.

Many interesting hats were shared during *H* week.

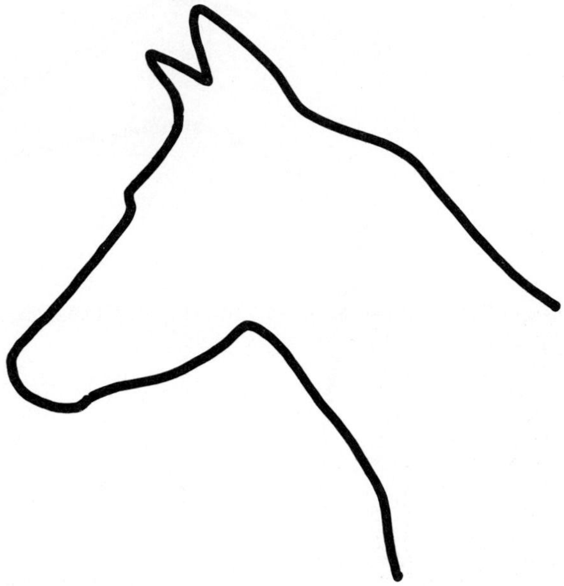

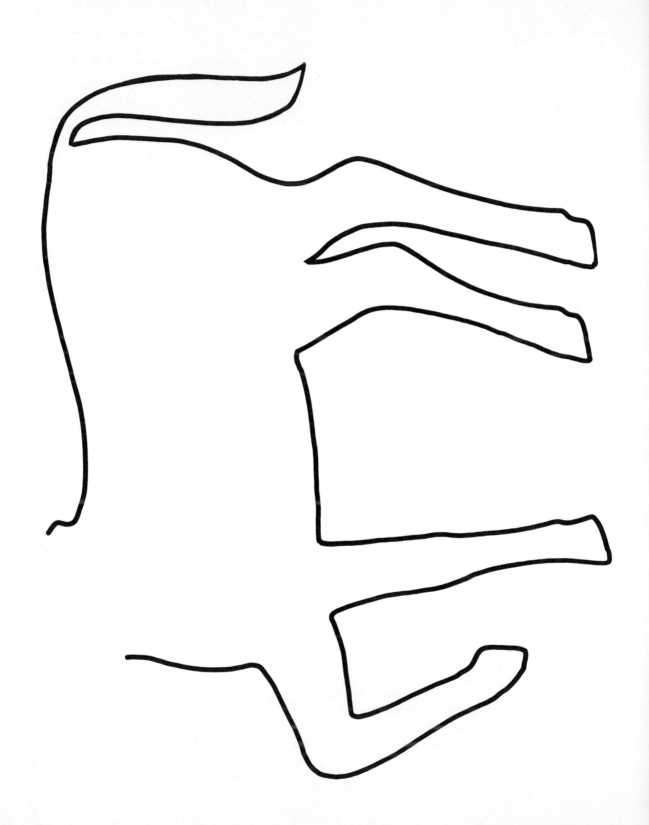

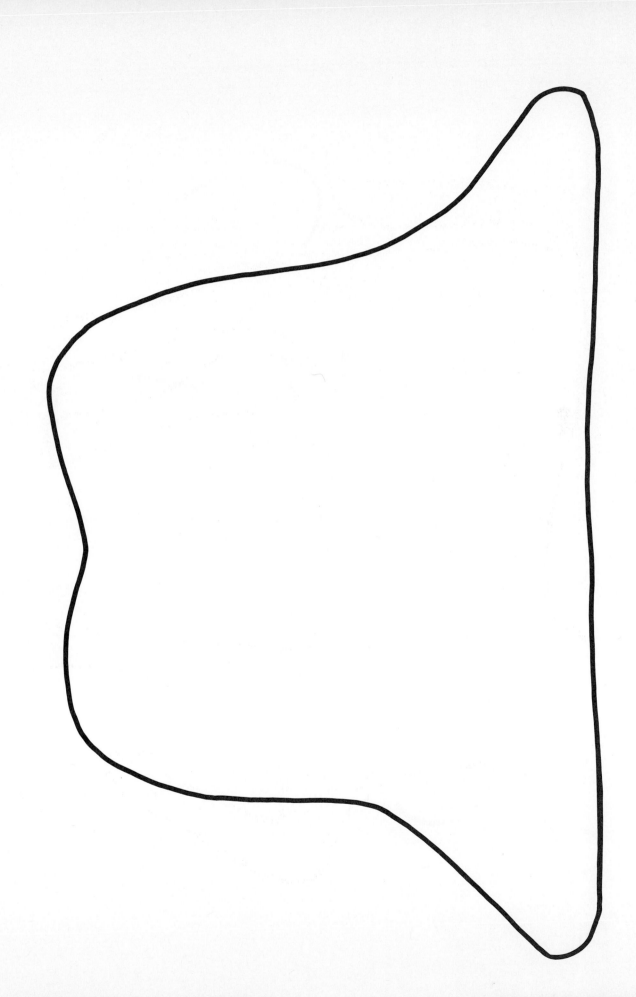

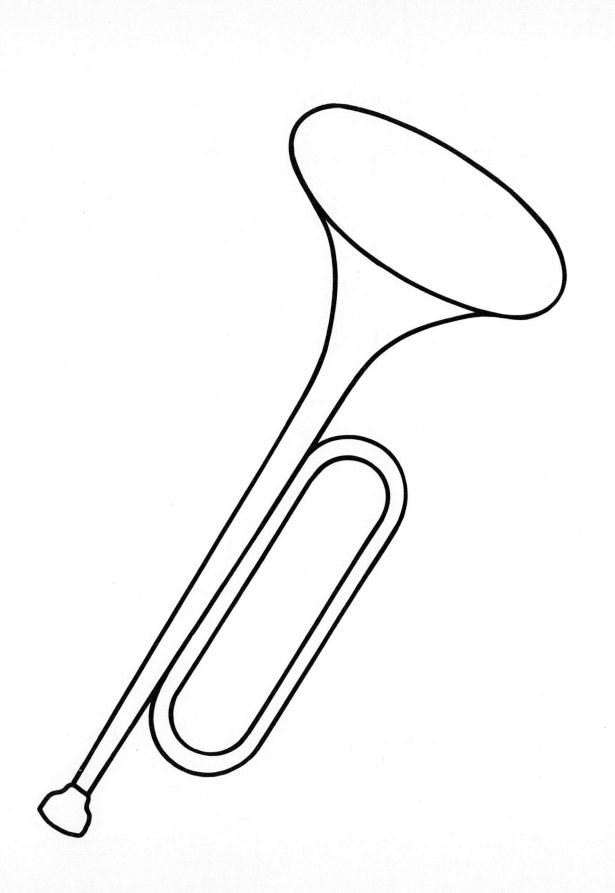

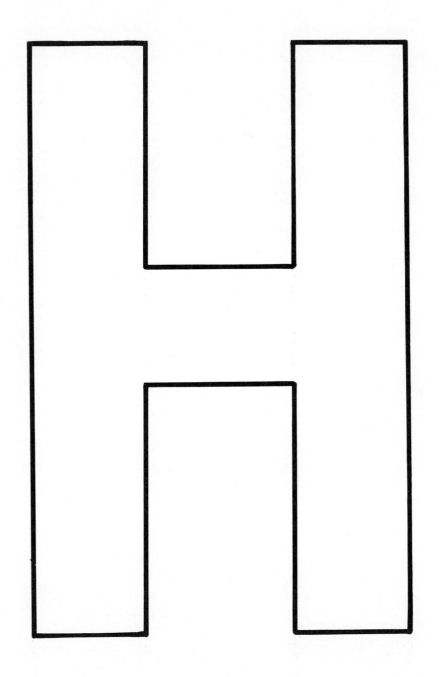

Visual closure card: *H*/Golden letter 107

I i

igloo (See pattern, page 114.)

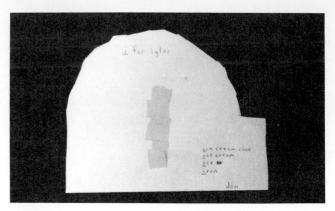

Igloo Letter Project

Letter bag items*

igloo   infant
iguana   ink
inch   insect
inchworm   instrument
Indian   invitation

Multisensory letter projects

iguana (See pattern, page 113.)

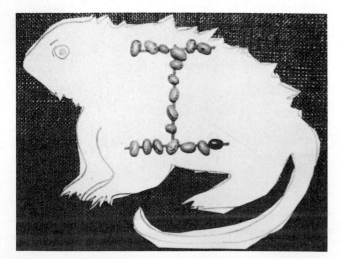

Iguana Letter Project

*When vowels are introduced, the short sound is emphasized, but we discuss with the children that letters often have other sounds.

Other projects

ink blot pictures

important books (Modeled after Margaret Wise Brown's book)

- Have children dictate or write and illustrate the completion of "The important thing about _____ is . . . ." Then put the pages together in a book.

creative insects

- All insects have six legs, bodies made up of head, thorax, and abdomen, and antennae. Children can put these parts together and decorate them as they wish.

invitations

initials

Thinking skills

Comprehension:

- Have children listen to the sounds made by various instruments and look at, touch carefully, and describe them.

- Discuss the concept in/out.

- Use visual closure cards. (See examples, pages 115–118.)

- Provide a set of insects for children to explore. Note similarities and differences with them.

- Study Indians.

Memory:

- Use memory book with pictures of insects.

  Designate "magic" pages in books that are read.

Decision making:

- Have children classify instruments by sight, sound, or both. Discuss the classifications.
- Have children classify insects. Discuss the classifications.
- Have children classify invitations. Discuss the classifications.

Creativity:

- Have children brainstorm flavors of ice cream or things to do in icy weather.

Food projects

Ice cream (*Cook and Learn*)
Irish soda bread (*Cook and Learn*)
Ironed sandwich (*Cook and Learn*)

Books

Arrow to the Sun: A Pueblo Indian Tale, by Gerald McDermott. New York: The Viking Press, 1974.

Important Book, by Margaret Wise Brown, illustrated by Leonard Weisgard. New York: Harper & Row, 1949.

Indian Bunny, by Ruth Bornstein. New York: Scholastic Inc., 1973.

The Indoor Noisy Book, by Margaret Wise Brown, illustrated by Leonard Weisgard. New York: W. R. Scott, 1942.

Ira Sleeps Over, by Bernard Waber. Boston: Houghton Mifflin, 1972.

Knots on a Counting Rope, by Bill Martin, Jr., illustrated by Joe Smith. New York: Holt, Rinehart and Winston, 1966.

Let's Look at Insects, by Deboarah Manley, illustrated by Annabel Milne and Peter Stebbing. New York: Derrydale, 1977.

The Trees Stand Shining, Poetry of the American Indians, selected by Hettie Jones, illustrated by Robert Andrew Parker. New York: Dial Press, 1971.

When Clay Sings, by Byrd Baylor, illustrated by Tom Bahti. New York: Charles Scribner's Sons, 1972.

Songs and fingerplays

Insect Parts
Head, thorax, abdomen,
Head, thorax, abdomen,
Head, thorax, abdomen,
Two antennae and six little legs,
Head, thorax, abdomen.

–Author unknown–

Science projects

Melt ice.
Study insects.
Make instruments.

Field trips and visitors

music store or conservatory (to see instruments)
infant
intern

Children demonstrated the concept *in.*

Multisensory letter project: iguana 113

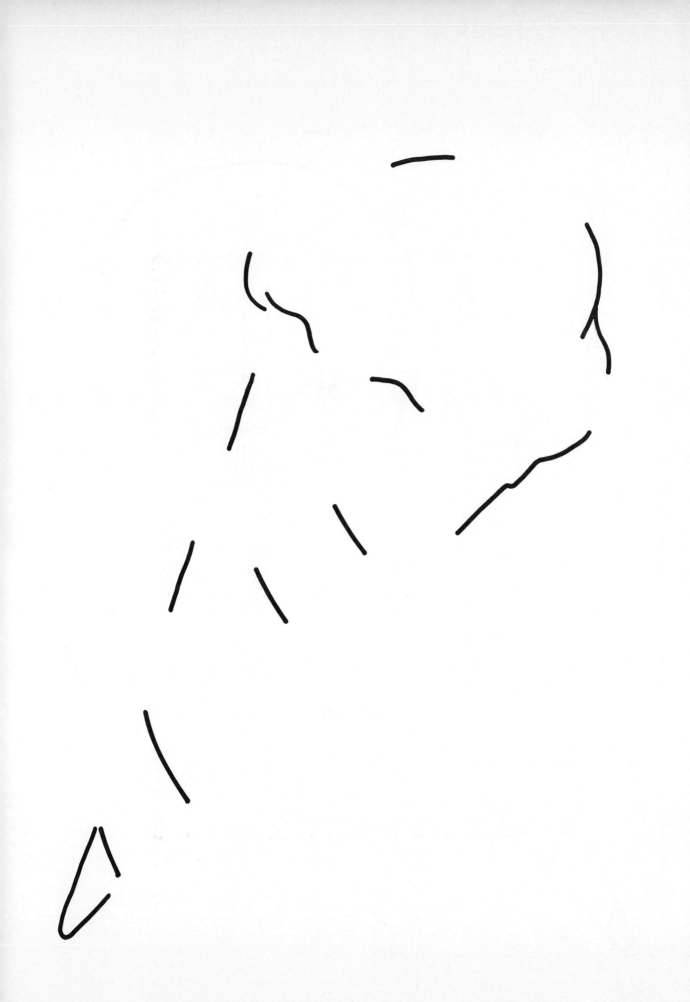

116 Visual closure card: ice cream cone

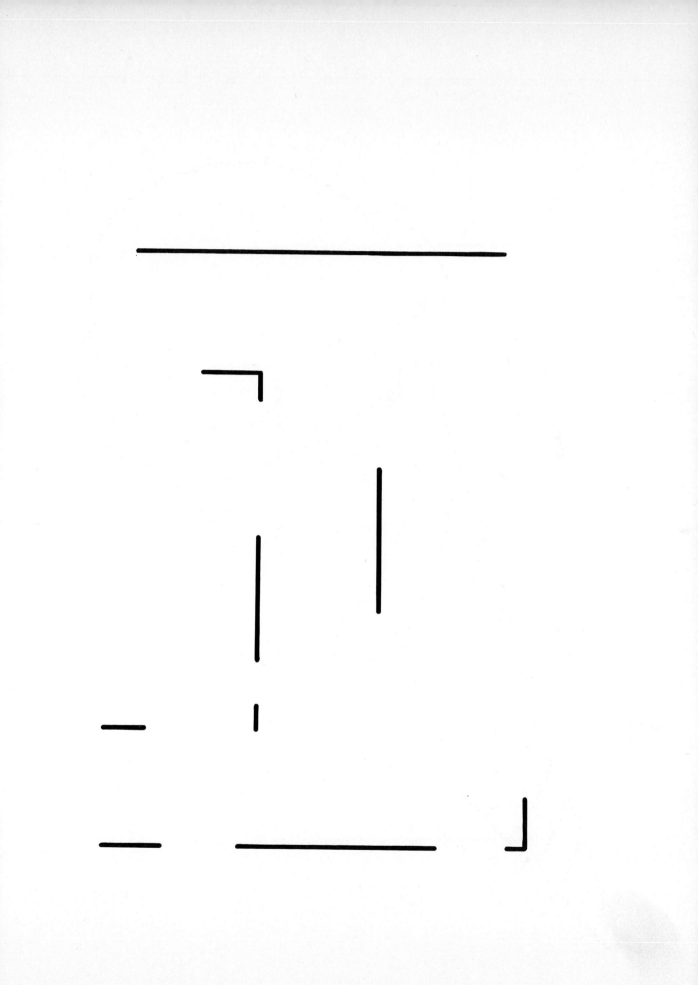

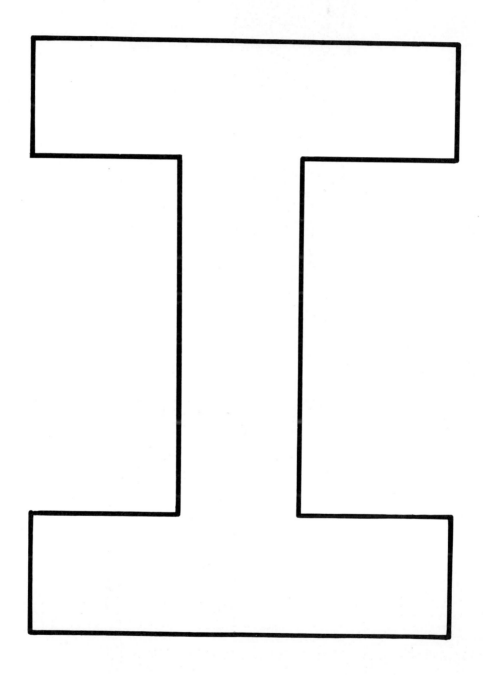

J j

Jj

Jelly bean jar (See pattern, page 124.)

Jelly Bean Jar Letter Project

Letter bag items

jack-in-the-box	jeep
jack-o-lantern	jelly bean
jacket	jet
jacks	jewelry
Japanese doll	jig saw puzzle
jar	juice
jeans	jump rope

Multisensory letter projects

jack-in-the-box (See pattern, page 123.)

■ Fold construction paper four inches from top. Place "Jack" under fold. Open at fold to see Jack's head.

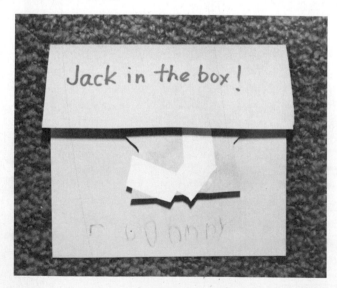

Jack-in-the-box Letter Project

Other projects

jewelry (macaroni necklaces, etc.)

junk sculpture

jungle animals made from clay

jungle diorama

jig saw puzzle

■ Have children draw pictures, cut them into pieces, and try to reassemble them.

jet from paper

Thinking skills

Comprehension:

■ Use visual closure cards. (See examples, pages 125–128.)

■ Provide one of the following sets of objects for children to explore: jewelry, junk, jungle animals, jackets, or jars. Have them touch, smell, and describe the items.

■ Ask children to share jokes and jingles.

■ Have children learn about Japan.

A mother shared Japanese crafts with the children.

Memory:
- Use the memory tray with items from the letter bag.
- Use the memory book with pictures of different foods in jars.
- Play *Concentration* using cards made with jungle animal stickers.
- Designate "magic" pages in books that are read.

Decision making:
- Have children classify the items in one of the following groups: jewelry, junk, jungle animals, jackets, jars. Discuss the classifications.
- Make a juice graph. (Children choose a favorite juice from a selection of three or more. They then place a symbol for their favorite juice on the graph. When all have chosen, the group discusses the findings.)

Creativity:
- Have children brainstorm pictures that could be on a jig-saw puzzle.
- Let children act out the story *Jack and the Beanstalk* or the rhymes *Jack and Jill* and *Jack Be Nimble.*

Food Projects

juice (*Cook and Learn*)
Japanese cuisine
jam sandwiches
jam or jelly

Books

Bread and Jam for Frances, by Russell Hoban. New York: Harper & Row, 1964.

Giant Jam Sandwich, by John Vernon Lord, with verses by Janet Burroway. Boston: Houghton Mifflin, 1973.

Jack and the Beanstalk, by William Stobbs. New York: Delacorte Press, 1965.

Jamberry, by Bruce Degen. New York: Harper & Row, 1983.

Jelly Book, by Ralph Steadman. New York: Scroll Press, 1970.

Jennie's Hat, by Ezra Jack Keats. New York: Harper & Row, 1966.

Jingle Bells, by Kathleen N. Daly, illustrated by J. P. Miller. Racine, Wis.: Golden Press.

Journey Cake, Ho! by Ruth Sawyer, illustrated by Robert McCloskey. New York: The Viking Press, 1953.

Jump Frog Jump, by Robert Kalan. New York: Greenwillow Books, 1981.

Jungle Jumble, by Barbara Bartocci, illustrated by Rosalyn Schanzer. Kansas City, Mo.: Hallmark.

One-Eyed Jake, by Pat Hutchins. New York: Greenwillow Books, 1979.

This Is the House That Jack Built. Illustrated by Iris Simon. New York: Dandelion Press, 1979.

Wake Up, Jeremiah, by Ronald Himler. New York: Harper & Row, 1979.

Songs and fingerplays

Jack and Jill

Jack Be Nimble

Two Little Blackbirds
Two little blackbirds
Sitting on a hill
One named Jack,
One named Jill.
Fly away, Jack.
Fly away, Jill.
Come back, Jack.
Come back, Jill.
(The hands are used to show the motions of the birds.)

—Author unknown—

Science project

Plant bean seeds, as in *Jack and the Beanstalk.*

Field trips and visitors

junk yard
jewelry shop
jet pilot
jazz musician

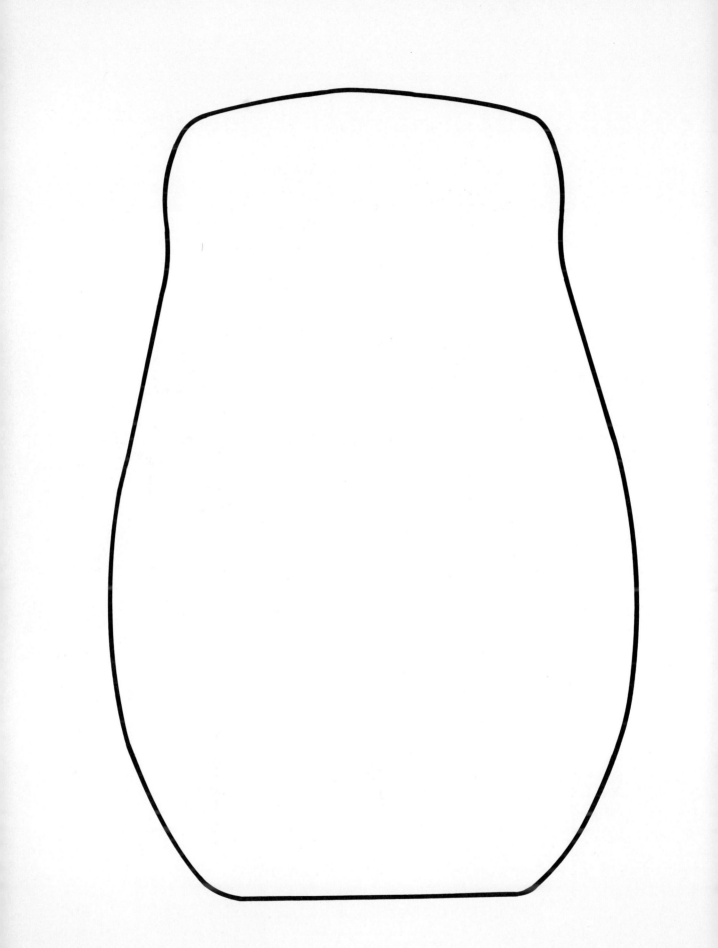

126 Visual closure card: jack-in-the-box

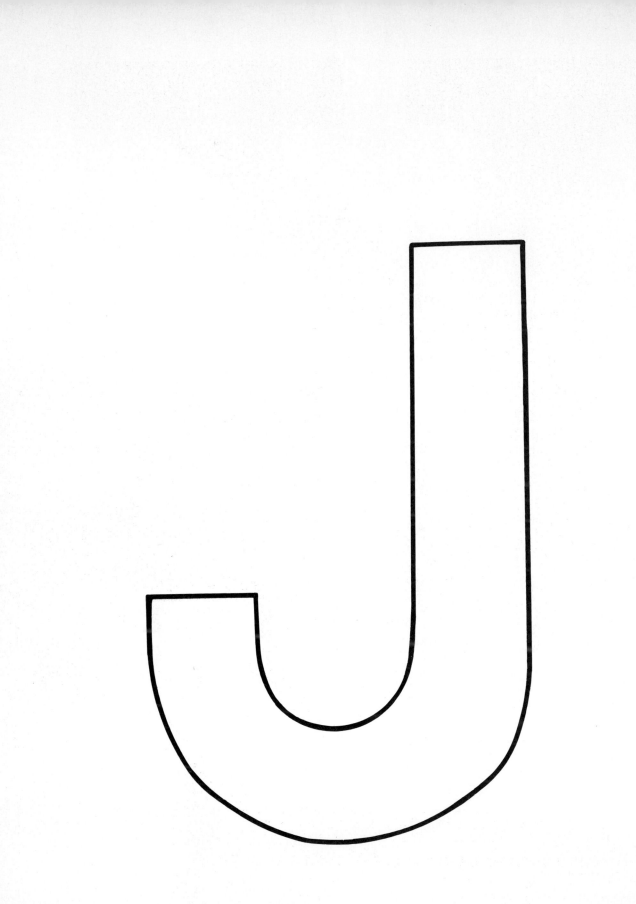

K k

129

K k

kite (See pattern, page 134.)

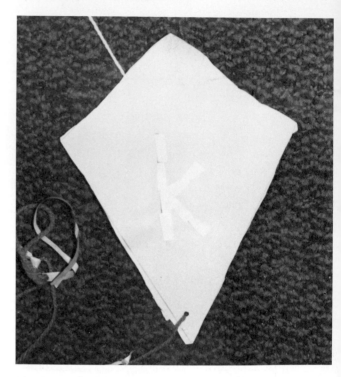

Kite Letter Project

Letter bag items

kangaroo	king
kayak	kit
ketchup	kitchen
kettle	kite
key	kitten
kimono	koala

Multisensory letter projects

kangaroo (See pattern, page 133.)

Kangaroo Letter Project

Other projects

king's crown

kitchen gadget printing

kitchen collage

- Have children cut pictures of kitchen items from magazines and paste them on paper.

kiss prints

- Apply lipstick to children with individual cotton swabs and have them print kisses on light-colored paper.

Thinking skills

Comprehension:

- Provide a set of keys for children to explore. Ask them to touch, look at, and describe their characteristics.

- Let children explore a set of kitchen gadgets. Ask what they are and what they might do. Note their characteristics.

- Use visual closure cards. (See examples, pages 135–138.)

- Have children observe a kitten and find out about what it likes and what it does.

Memory:
- Use the memory book with pictures of objects from a kitchen.
- Designate "magic" pages in books that are read.

Decision making:
- Have children classify the items in one of the following groups: keys, kittens, or kitchen things. Discuss the classifications.
- Have children classify magazine pictures according to whether or not the objects are usually found in a kitchen.
- Offer children three keys inside a sock. Have them try to determine by touch alone which two keys are alike.

Creativity:
- Have children brainstorm things found in the kitchen.
- Let children act out the rhyme about the *Three Little Kittens.*

Food projects

kuchen (adapted as biscuit covered with fruit)

kabob
- Let children thread cut pieces of apple, orange, banana on a straw.

Books

In the Night Kitchen, by Maurice Sendak. New York: Harper & Row, 1970.

Just in Time for the King's Birthday, by E. B. Chance, illustrated by Arline Meyer. New York: Scholastic Inc., 1970.

Katy-No-Pocket, by Emmy Payne, illustrated by H. A. Rey. New York: Scholastic Inc., 1972.

Kenny's Crazy Kite, by Arnold Shapiro, illustrated by Karen Acosta. Los Angeles: Price/Stern/Sloan, 1978.

My Kitchen, by Harlow Rockwell. New York: Greenwillow Books, 1980.

What Do You Do With a Kangaroo? by Mercer Mayer. New York: Scholastic Inc., 1973.

Songs and fingerplays

Kookaburra
Kookaburra sits on an old gum tree.
Merry, merry king of the bush is he.
Laugh, Kookaburra, laugh, Kookaburra.
Gay your life must be.

–Author unknown–

(Note: A kookaburra is an Australian snake-killing bird with a strange call.)

Science project

Observe kites in the wind.

Field trips and visitors

commercial kitchen
kite store
kennel

Exploration of kitchen gadgets was a favorite activity.

Multisensory letter project: kangaroo 133

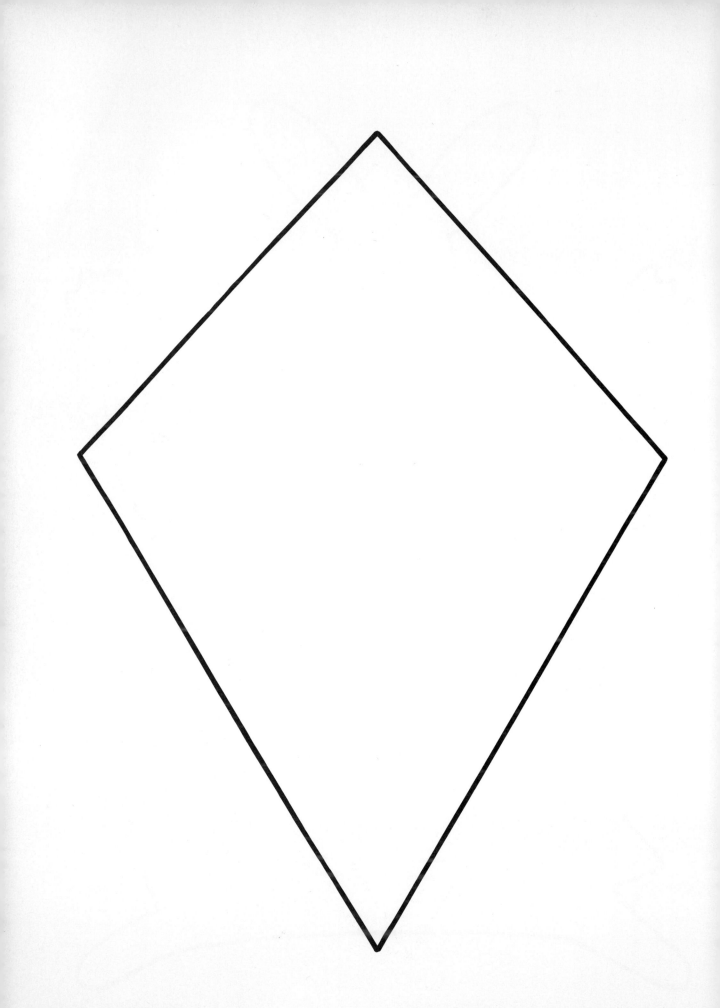

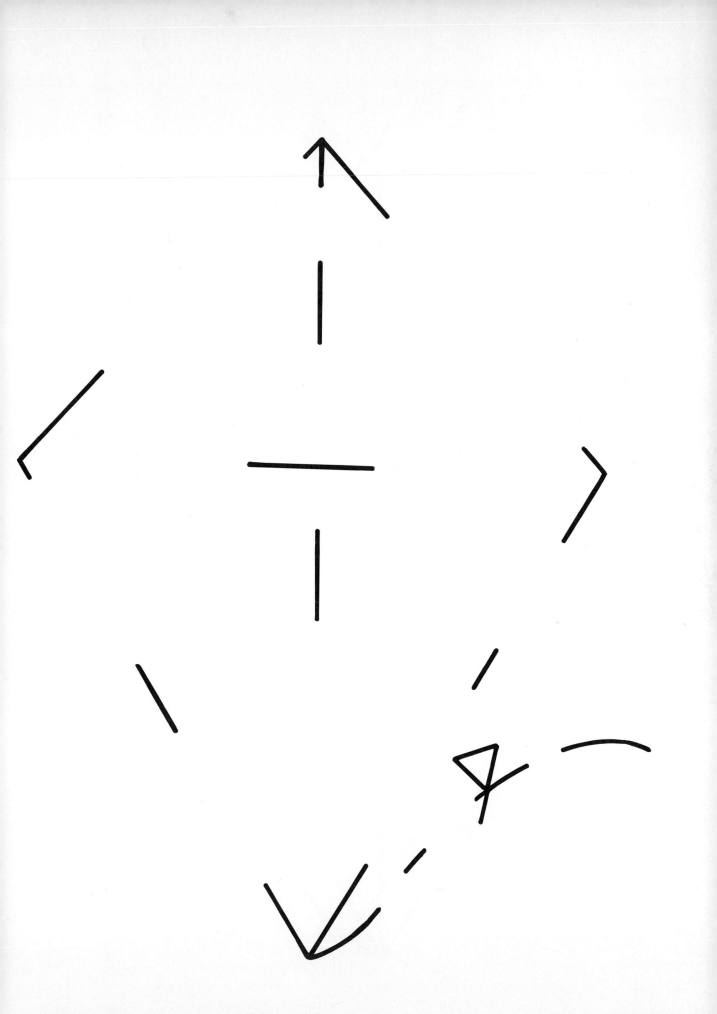

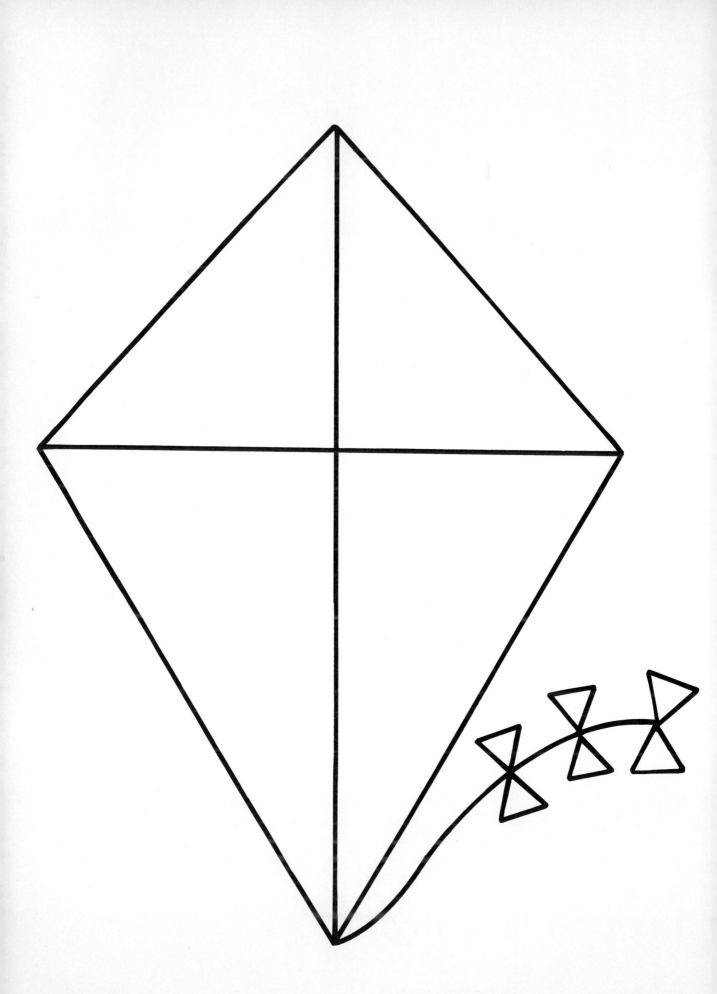

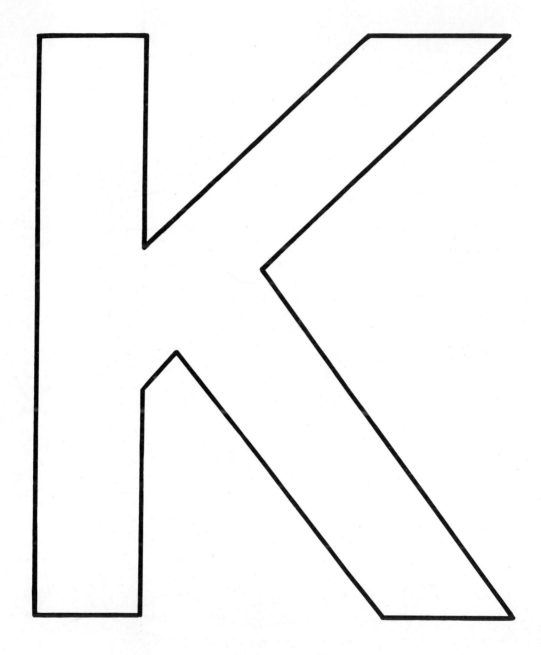

138 Visual closure card: *K*/Golden letter

L l

Letter bag items

label	lemon
lace	lid
ladder	lightbulb
ladle	lion
ladybug	lizard
lamb	lobster
leaf	lunch box

Multisensory letter projects

lips (See pattern, page 143.)

Lips Letter Project

lion (See pattern, pages 144–145.)

Lion Letter Project

Other projects

L collage

Children worked on *L* collages.

lion puppet

- Paste circle face on small paper bag. Have children add yarn for the mane and draw features.

lines (using rulers)

leis (from egg carton sections)

letters (dictated to an adult or written by children)

leaf rubbings

lace collage

love collage

- Have children cut out pictures for a collage of things that they love, and dictate or write stories about the collage.

linoleum block prints

Thinking skills

Comprehension:

- Provide one of the following sets of objects for children to explore: alphabet letters, leaves, labels, lids, locks, or lace. Have them touch, smell, and describe the items.

- Have children listen to noises and try to identify them by sound alone.
- Discuss with children the following concepts: loud/soft, left/right, and last/first.
- Use visual closure cards. (See examples, pages 146–149.)

Memory:
- Use the memory tray with items from the letter bag.
- Use the memory book.
- Let children play *Concentration* using cards made from food labels.
- Designate "magic" pages in books that are read.

Decision making:
- Have children classify items in one of the following sets: alphabet letters, leaves, labels, lids, locks, or lace. Discuss the classifications.
- Ask children to match locks with keys.
- Ask children to match lids with containers.
- Ask children to sort laundry.

Creativity:
- Have children brainstorm objects that fit in in a lunch box.

Food projects

lumpia (meat and vegetable rolls from the Philippines)
lunch
lasagna
lemonade (*Cook and Learn*)
latke (*Cook and Learn*)

Books

Around and Around—Love, by Betty Miles. New York: Alfred A. Knopf, 1975.

The Grouchy Ladybug, by Eric Carle. New York: Scholastic Inc., 1977.

If You Listen, by Charlotte Zolotow, illustrated by Marc Simont. New York: Harper & Row, 1980.

Leo the Late Bloomer, by Robert Kraus. New York: Windmill Books, 1971.

Leo the Lop, by Stephen Cosgrove, illustrated by Robin James. Bothell, Wash.: Serendipity Press, 1977.

A Letter to Amy, by Ezra Jack Keats. New York: Harper & Row, 1968.

Light, by Donald Crews. New York: Greenwillow Books, 1981.

Lovable Lyle, by Bernard Waber. Boston: Houghton Mifflin, 1969.

We'll Have a Friend for Lunch, by Jane Flory, illustrated by Carolyn Croll. Boston: Houghton Mifflin, 1974.

Songs and fingerplays

Here We Go Looby Loo
   (Place a sticker on each child's left hand.)

Mary Had a Little Lamb

Did You Ever See A Lassie?

Little Bo-Peep

London Bridge

Leaves
Like a leaf and a feather
In the windy weather
We will whirl and twirl about
And then sink down together.

–Author unknown–

Science projects

Sprout lima beans.
Study leaves.

Field trips and visitors

laundromat
letter carrier
librarian
library
lifeguard

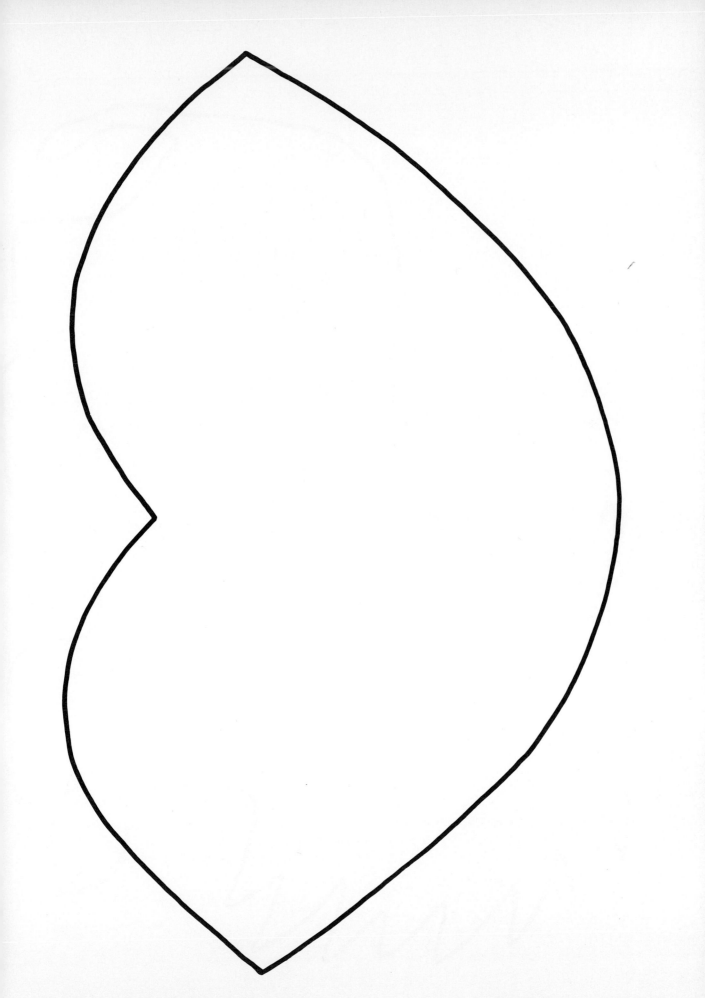

144 Multisensory letter project: lion (body)

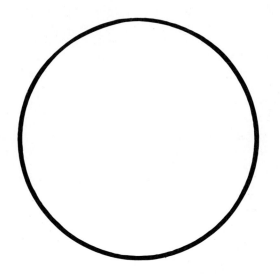

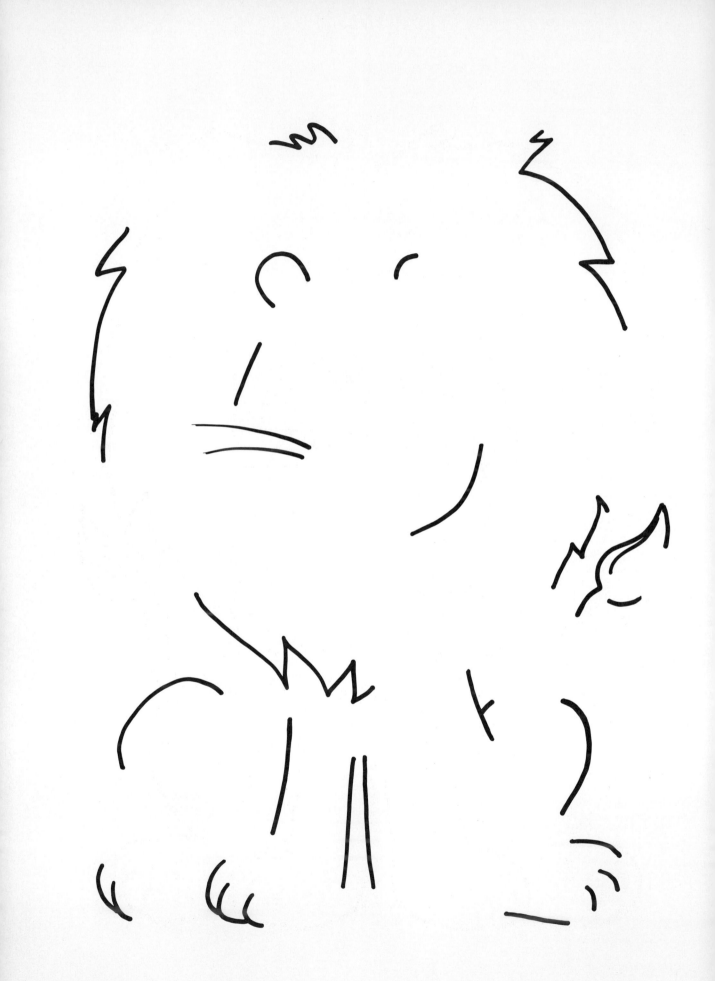

Visual closure card: lion 147

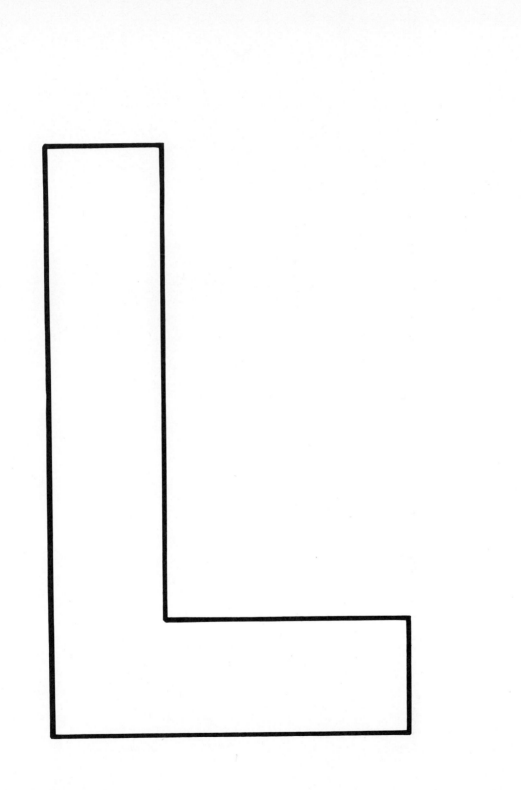

Visual closure card: *L*/Golden letter 149

M m

Mm

mitten (See pattern, page 156.)

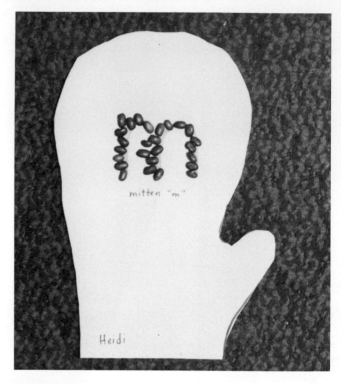

Mitten Letter Project

Letter bag items

macaroni	mitten
magnet	monkey
map	monster
marble	moon
margarine	moose
mask	maracas
milk	moth
mirror	mouse

Multisensory letter projects

mouse (See pattern, page 155; use yarn for tail.)

Mouse Letter Project

Other projects

marching

macaroni collage

masks

mazes

monsters

- Have children dictate or write and illustrate a story about monsters they would like to know.

mobile

maracas

marble painting

- Place paper in a large, shallow box. Show children how to dip marbles in paint and tilt the box so that the marbles roll across the paper.

Thinking skills

Comprehension:

- Have children study Mexico.

- Ask children to observe the action of magnets.
- Provide mirrors for children to look inside their mouths.
- Provide a variety of music for children to listen to.
- Ask children to taste and compare various melons. Have them observe the outside, inside, seeds, texture, size, etc. (If melons are not in season, children could taste and compare different muffins.)
- Use visual closure cards. (See examples, pages 157–160.)
- Have children study money.
- Have children use materials to depict the concept more/less.

Memory:
- Use the memory tray with items from the letter bag.
- Use the memory book.
- Designate "magic" pages in books that are read.

Decision making:
- Have children classify items in one of the following sets: marbles, macaroni, money, masks, mittens, and men. Discuss the classifications.
- Ask children to arrange money (coins) in sequence from largest to smallest in size and then value.
- Play music. Have children classify selections according to speed, volume, and other characteristics.

Creativity:
- Have children brainstorm things that magnets attract.

Food projects

milkshake (*Cook and Learn*)
muffins (*Cook and Learn*)
macaroni salad (*Cook and Learn*)
melon balls
mayonnaise
African meatballs (*Cook and Learn*)

Books

Animals Born Alive and Well, by Ruth Heller. New York: Grosset and Dunlap, 1982.

Are You My Mother? by P. D. Eastman. New York: Random House, 1960.

The Awful Mess, by Anne Rockwell. New York: Parents Magazine Press, 1973.

City Mouse–Country Mouse, illustrated by Marian Parry. New York: Scholastic Inc., 1970.

Madeline, by Ludwig Bemelmans. New York: Scholastic Inc., 1939.

Maggie and the Pirate, by Ezra Jack Keats. New York: Scholastic Inc., 1979.

The Magic Mirror Book and *Magic Mirror Tricks,* by Marion Walter. New York: Scholastic Inc., 1971.

The Marvelous Mud Washing Machine, by Patty Wolcott, illustrated by Richard Brown. New York: Scholastic Inc., 1974.

McBroom and the Beanstalk, by Sid Fleischman, illustrated by Walter Lorraine. Boston: Little, Brown and Company, 1978.

Mike Mulligan and His Steam Shovel, by Virginia Lee Burton. New York: Houghton Mifflin, 1939.

Mother, Mother, I Want Another, by Maria Polushkin, illustrated by Diane Dawson. New York: Scholastic Inc., 1978.

The Mouse Book, by Helen Piers. New York: Scholastic Inc., 1966.

Mouse Soup, by Arnold Lobel. New York: Harper & Row, 1977.

Mouse Work, by Robert Kraus, illustrated by Jose Aruego and Ariane Dewey. New York: Windmill, 1980.

On Market Street, by Arnold Lobel, illustrated by Anita Lobel. New York: Scholastic Inc., 1981.

The Story of a Little Mouse Trapped in a Book, by Monique Felix. La Jolla, Calif.: Green Tiger Press, 1980.

Tell Me a Mitzi, by Lore Segal, illustrated by Harriet Pincus. New York: Farrar, Straus, and Giroux, 1970.

Thidwick: The Big Hearted Moose, by Dr. Seuss. New York: Random House, 1948.

1000 Monsters, by Alan Benjamin, illustrated by Sal Murdocca. New York: Scholastic Inc., 1979.

Whose Mouse Are You? by Robert Kraus, illustrated by Jose Aruego. New York: Macmillan Company, 1970.

Songs and fingerplays

Five Little Monkeys
Five little monkeys jumping on the bed—
One fell off and bumped his head.
Went to the doctor and the doctor said,
"No more monkeys jumping on the bed."
—Author unknown—

Do You Know the Muffin Man?

Merrily We Roll Along

Science projects

Study mammals.
Use magnets.
Learn magic tricks.

Field trips and visitors

market
museum
music shop
mail carrier
musicians
mechanic

Children classified marbles in many different ways.

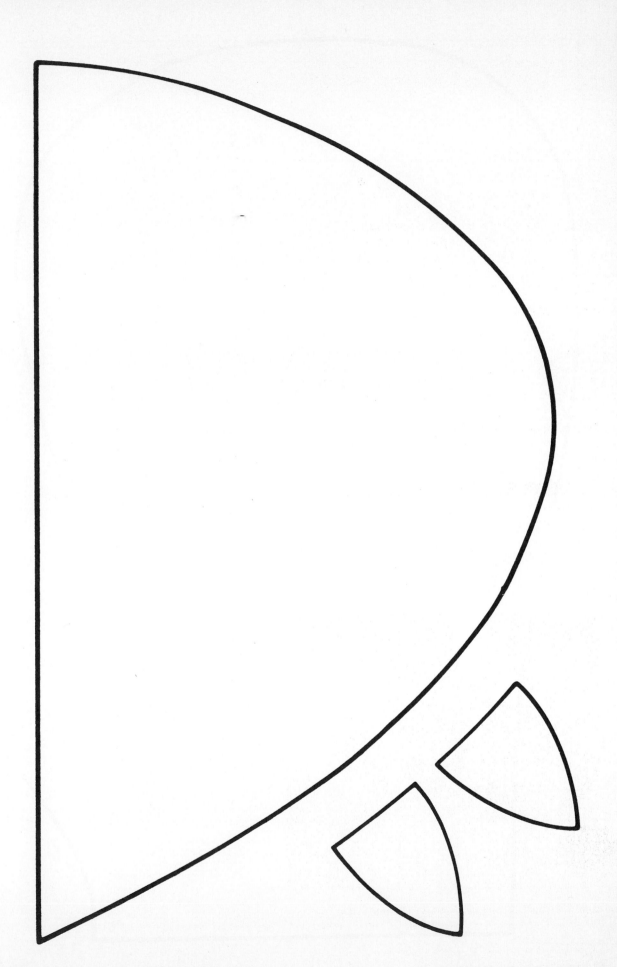

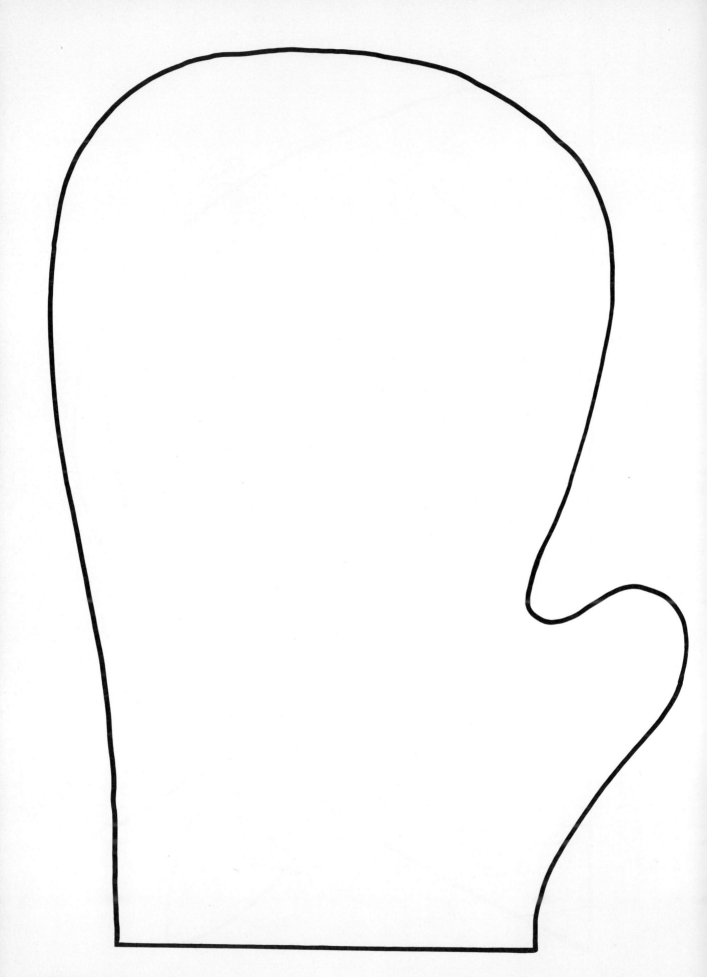

156 Multisensory letter project: mitten

158 Visual closure card: mitten

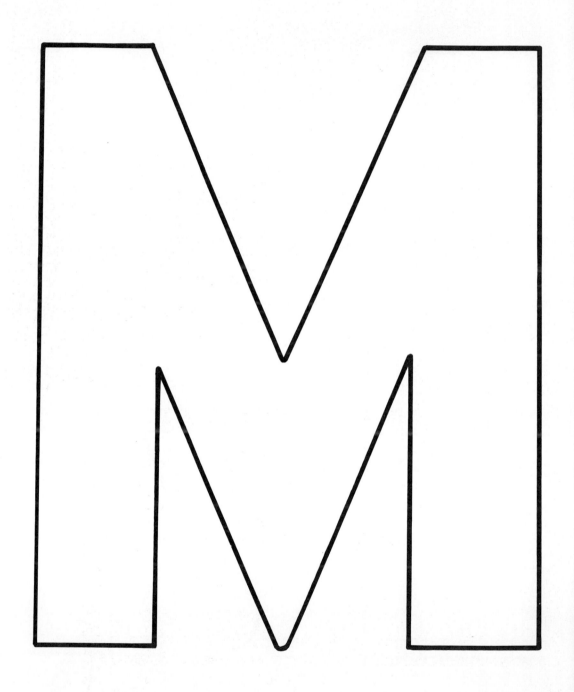

160 Visual closure card: *M*/Golden letter

Nn

Letter bag items

nail	newspaper
necklace	nickel
necktie	nine
needle	noodle
nest	nurse
net	nut

Multisensory letter projects

N necklace (Use visual closure *N* as pattern, page 168.)

newspaper n

Newspaper *n* Letter Project

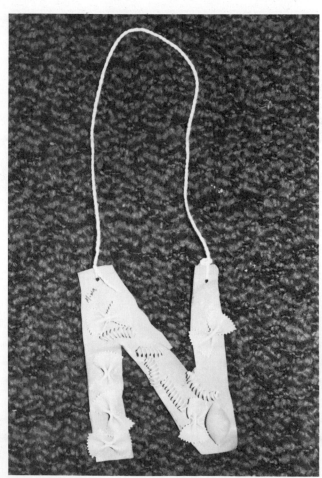

N Necklace Letter Project

Other projects

necklaces

nests

- Mix pine needles or shredded wheat and white glue. Mold into nest shape. Let dry and have children fill the nests with eggs made from cornstarch dough.

Nest

needlework (yarn on burlap)

noodle collage

name cards

- Print each child's name on cardboard. Cover the name with glue. Have children sprinkle sand on the glue to make a name card with an interesting texture.

Thinking skills

Comprehension:

- Have children use their noses to explore a smell kit. Saturate cotton with flavorings, such as vanilla, orange, maple, almond, chocolate. Or have children smell different spices and describe the smells.

- Have children explore the neighborhood.

- Have children study neighborhood helpers.

- Provide different types of nests for children to examine.

- Ask children to listen to different noises.

- Use visual closure cards. (See examples, pages 165–168.)

- Have children taste, smell, look at, feel, and describe different nuts on a nut tasting tray.

Memory:

- Let children play *Concentration* using the names of the children in the class on the cards.

- Use the memory book with pictures of neighborhood helpers.

- Designate "magic" pages in books that are read.

Decision making:

- Have children classify noises according to whether they are loud or soft, near or far.

- Have children classify a set of nuts of different varieties. Discuss the classifications.

- Let children match objects and neighborhood helpers to their appropriate setting (food to clerk in grocery store, etc.)

- Ask children to classify activities according to whether they take place during the night or during the day.

Creativity:

- Have children brainstorm things that make noise.

- Let children act out nursery rhymes.

Food projects

nut tasting

navy bean soup

noodles

nachos

- Lay tortilla chips in a single layer on a cookie sheet. Sprinkle with grated cheese and bake in a 400° oven until cheese melts (about 5 minutes).

Books

A Bag Full of Nothing, by Jay Williams, illustrated by Tom O'Sullivan. New York: Parents Magazine Press, 1974.

Good Night 1, 2, 3, by Yutaka Sugita. New York: Scroll Press, 1971.

Goodnight, Moon, by Margaret Wise Brown, illustrated by Clement Hurd. New York: Harper & Row, 1947.

Miss Nelson Is Missing, by Harry Allard and James Marshall. Boston: Houghton Mifflin, 1977.

Night Animals, by Millicent E. Selsam. New York: Scholastic Inc., 1979.

Nightdances, by James Skofield, illustrated by Karen Gundersheimer. New York: Harper & Row, 1981.

Night Noises, and Other Mole and Troll Stories, by Tony Johnston, illustrated by Cyndy Szekeres. New York: G. P. Putnam's Sons, 1977.

Noisy Nora, by Rosemary Wells. New York: Scholastic Inc., 1973.

Nothing at All, by Wanda Gag. New York: Coward, McCann, and Geoghegan, 1941.

1 Hunter, by Pat Hutchins. New York: Greenwillow Books, 1982.

Too Much Noise, by Ann McGovern, illustrated by Simms Taback. New York: Scholastic Inc., 1967.

There's a Nightmare in My Closet, by Mercer Mayer. New York: Dial Press, 1968.

Songs and fingerplays

Who Are the People in My Neighborhood?
  (from Sesame Street)

Number songs, such as
Ten Little Indians
This Old Man

Number rhymes, such as
One, Two, Buckle My Shoe
One, two, buckle my shoe.
Three, four, shut the door.
Five, six, pick up sticks.
Seven, eight, lay them straight.
Nine, ten, a big fat hen.

–Author unknown–

Science projects

Study the nesting of animals.
Study night animals.

Field trips and visitors

neighborhood stores or other locales
newspaper
nurse

Children explored number and pattern.

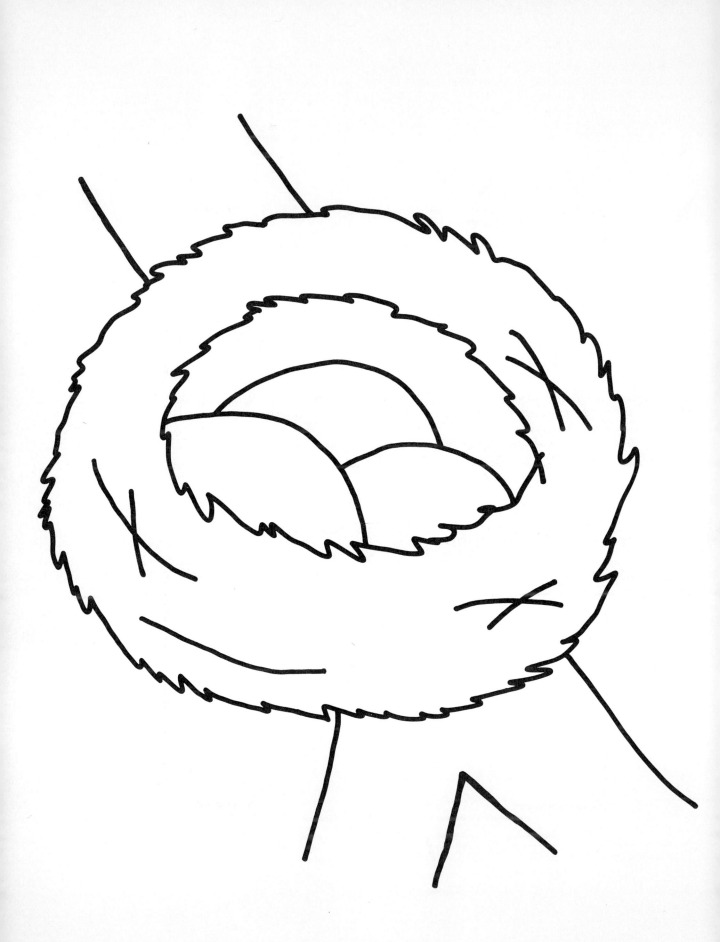

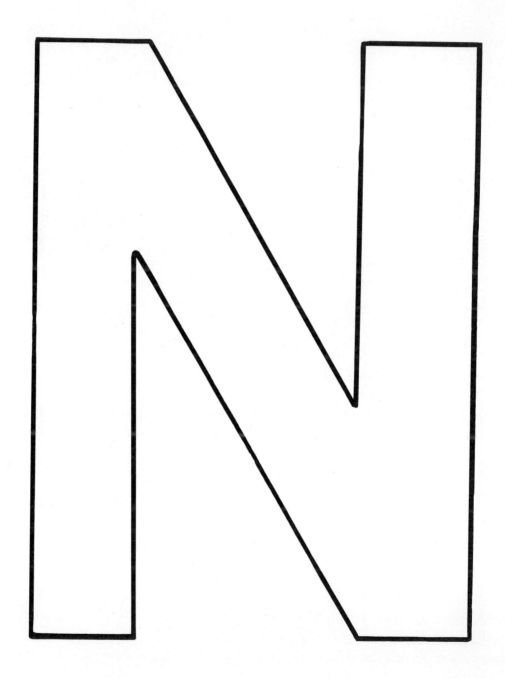

O o

ostrich (See pattern, page 173.)

Ostrich Letter Project

Letter bag items*

ocarina	on-off switch
octagon	opposite
October	ostrich
octopus	otter
olive	ox
omelet	

Multisensory letter projects

octopus

- Have children trace a circle and then cut it out. Then place eight round stickers around the circle. Ask the children to paste on eight strips, which requires one-to-one correspondence. Finally, have children glue confetti on the letter O.

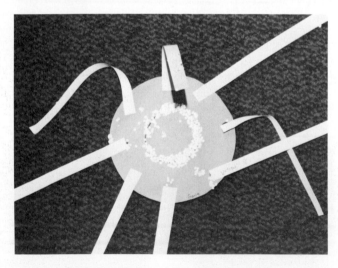

Octopus Letter Project

*When vowels are introduced, the short sound is emphasized, but we discuss with the children that letters often have other sounds.

Other projects

oval collage

string o-shaped cereal for necklaces

print with circles

oil and water prints

- Float oil on water colors in large flat pan. Have children dip the paper in the mixture to print.

opposite books

- Have children illustrate sets of opposites (in/out, etc.). Label the concepts and bind the illustrations into a book.

Thinking skills

Comprehension:

- Have children depict the meaning of the following concepts: open/closed, out/in, old/new, on/off.

- Ask children to demonstrate the meaning of opposites, such as up/down, in/out, go/stop, etc.

- Have children taste, smell, look at, feel, and describe a set of olives on an olive tasting tray.

- Ask children to taste different varieties of oranges, then compare and contrast.

- Use visual closure cards. (See examples, pages 174–175.)

Memory:

- Use the memory book with pictures of orange things.

- Use the memory tray.

- Designate "magic" pages in books that are read.

Decision making:

- Have children put oranges in sequence from largest to smallest.

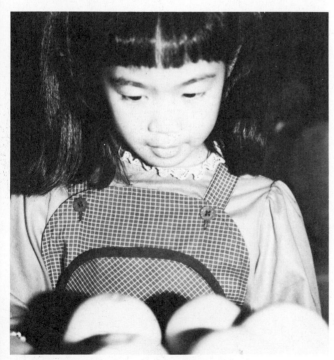

She studied the oranges carefully before she put them in sequence from largest to smallest.

- Have children classify different kinds of onions. Discuss the classifications.

Creativity:

- Have children brainstorm things found in the ocean.

Food projects

oatmeal—"Three Bear Porridge" (*Cook and Learn*)
omelet
orange juice
oatmeal sesame crisps (*Cook and Learn*)
oatmeal apple cookies (*Cook and Learn*)

Books

I Was All Thumbs, by Bernard Waber. Boston: Houghton Mifflin, 1975.

Oliver, by Syd Hoff. New York: Harper & Row, 1960.

Over in the Meadow, illustrated by Ezra Jack Keats, based on original by Olive A. Wadsworth. New York: Scholastic Inc., 1971.

Ox-Cart Man, by Donald Hall, illustrated by Barbara Cooney. New York: The Viking Press, 1979.

Thy Friend, Obadiah, by Brinton Turkle. New York: The Viking Press, 1969.

Traffic: A Book of Opposites, by Betsy and Giulio Maestro. New York: Crown, 1981.

Songs and fingerplays

Open, Shut Them
Open, shut them; open, shut them.
Give a little clap.
Open, shut them; open, shut them.
Lay them in your lap.
Creep them, creep them, creep them, creep them.
Right up to your chin.
Open wide your little mouth
But do not let them in.
–Author unknown–

Old Gray Goose
Old King Cole

Science projects

Sprout oats.
Study the ocean.

Field trips and visitors

ocean
oceanographer
octogenarian

Multisensory letter project: ostrich 173

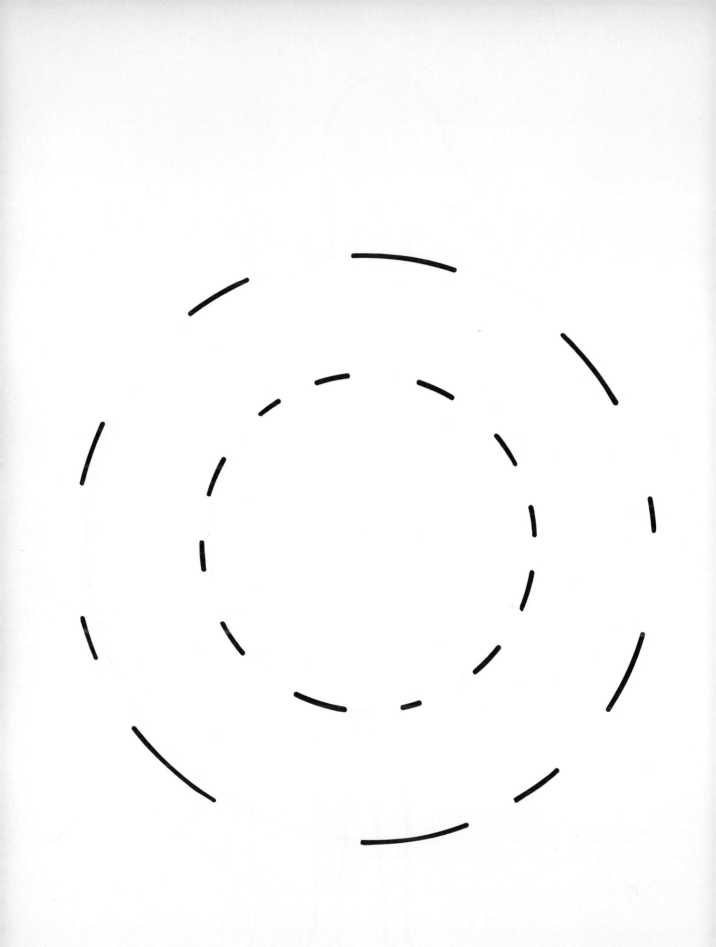

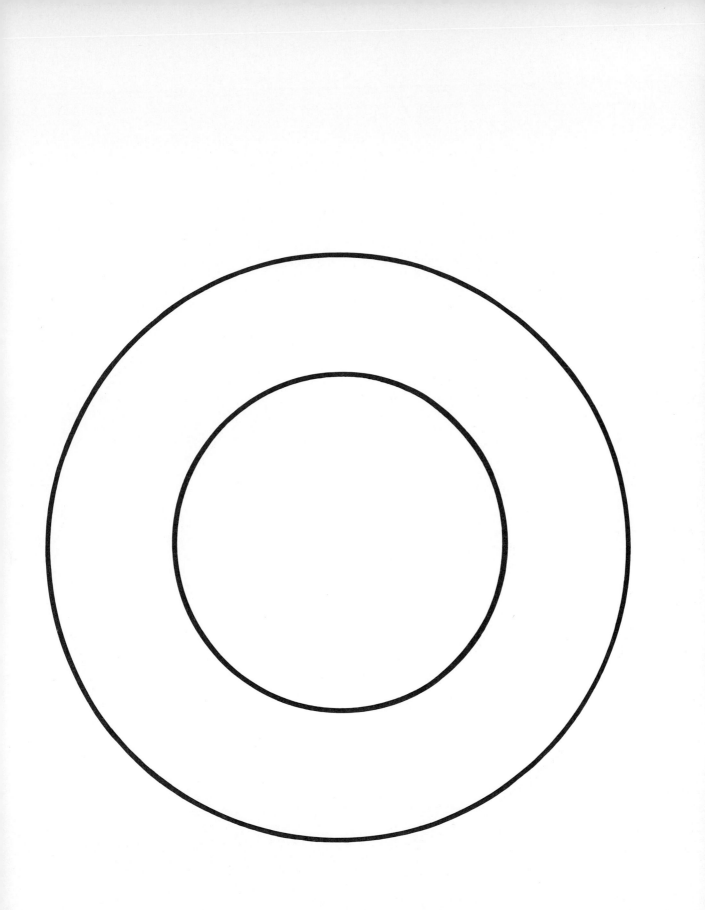

P p

P p

Letter bag items

panda	plate
pants	popcorn
pencil	porcupine
penguin	potato
penny	prism
pig	pumpkin
pink	puppet
pinwheel	

Multisensory letter projects

pumpkin (See pattern, page 181.)

Pumpkin Letter Project

pig (See pattern, pages 182–183.)

Pig Letter Project

Other projects

playdough

potato printing

puppets

patterns (from geometric shapes)

painting

paper collage

post office center

- Equip post office center with pencils, pens, stamps, paper, envelopes. Have children write or dictate letters and act out the mailing and delivery processes.

paper pizza

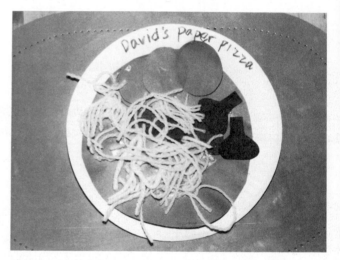

Paper Pizza Project

pinwheels

- Mark an *X* from corner to corner on a square piece of paper. Cut on the lines almost to the center. Help children attach every other corner piece to the center. Fasten a pin through the center of the pinwheel into the eraser of an unsharpened pencil.

Thinking skills

Comprehension:

- Have children observe various types of patterns, both visual and sound.

- Have children explore a pumpkin, outside and inside. Have them touch, smell, taste, and describe it.

- Use visual closure cards. (See examples, pages 184–187.)
- Help children learn about dangers from household poisons. (Obtain literature and stickers from a Poison Control Center.)
- Provide one of the following sets of objects for children to explore: paper, pens, people or pets. Have them describe the items.

Memory:

- Designate a "magic" page in books that are read.
- Use the memory tray with items from the letter bag.
- Use the memory book with pictures of various breeds of puppies.

Decision making:

- Prepare potatoes in various ways for children to taste (fried, mashed, raw, chips). Then have each child vote for the Positively Perfect Potato by placing a sticker in the appropriate column of a chart.

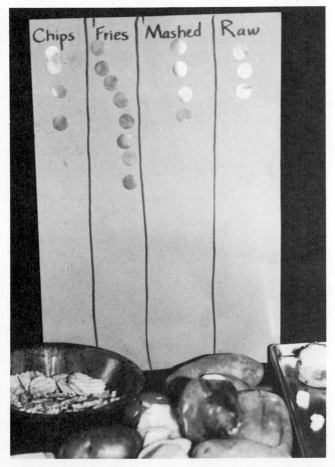

Potato Tasting Graph

- Ask children to reproduce patterns of hand claps (clap, pause, clap, clap; etc.).
- Have children classify one of the following sets: paper, pens, people or pets. Discuss the classifications.

Creativity:

- Let children act out the story of the *Three Little Pigs.*
- Have children brainstorm pink things or different ways to use paper.

Food projects

peanut butter (*Cook and Learn*)
popcorn
pasta
pineapple
pizza (*Cook and Learn*)
potato pancakes (latkes) (*Cook and Learn*)
cheese pretzels (*Cook and Learn*)

Books

The City Park, by Lothar Meggendorfer. New York: The Viking Press, 1981.

Each Peach Pear Plum, by Janet and Allan Ahlberg. New York: Scholastic Inc., 1978.

Papagayo: the Mischief Maker, by Gerald McDermott. New York: Windmill/Wanderer, 1980.

A Penguin Year, by Susan Bonners. New York: Delacorte Press, 1981.

Pickle, Pickle, Pickle Juice, by Patty Wolcott, illustrated by Blair Drawson. New York: Scholastic Inc., 1975.

Pierre: A Cautionary Tale in Five Chapters and a Prologue, by Maurice Sendak. New York: Scholastic Inc., 1962.

Pig Pig Grows Up, by David McPhail. New York: Scholastic Inc., 1980.

A Pocket for Corduroy, by Don Freeman. New York: Scholastic Inc., 1978.

Policemen, by Ina K. Dillon, illustrated by Robert Bartram. Chicago: Melmont, 1957.

The Story About Ping, by Marjorie Flack and Kurt Wiese. New York: The Viking Press, 1933, 1961.

Three Little Pigs, by Paul Galdone. New York: Scholastic Inc., 1970.

A Treeful of Pigs, by Arnold Lobel, illustrated by
Anita Lobel. New York: Scholastic Inc., 1979.

Songs and fingerplays

This Little Pig
This little pig went to market.
This little pig stayed home.
This little pig ate roast beef.
This little pig ate none.
And this little pig cried wee, wee, wee all the
    way home.
    *(Point to fingers or toes in turn, ending on
    the small one.)*
                                        –Author unknown–

Pancake
Mix a pancake,
Stir a pancake,
Pop it in a pan.
Fry a pancake,
Toss a pancake,
Catch it if you can.
                                        –Author unknown–

Peter Piper
Peter Piper picked a peck of pickled peppers.
A peck of pickled peppers Peter Piper picked.

Interesting animals came for the pet show.

Science projects

Grow a potato.
Experiment with a prism.
Make paper.
Grow plants.

Field trips and visitors

park
post office
pediatrician
pet store
pizza parlor
principal

Additional ideas

Have a pet show.

Multisensory letter project: pumpkin 181

Multisensory letter project: pig (body)

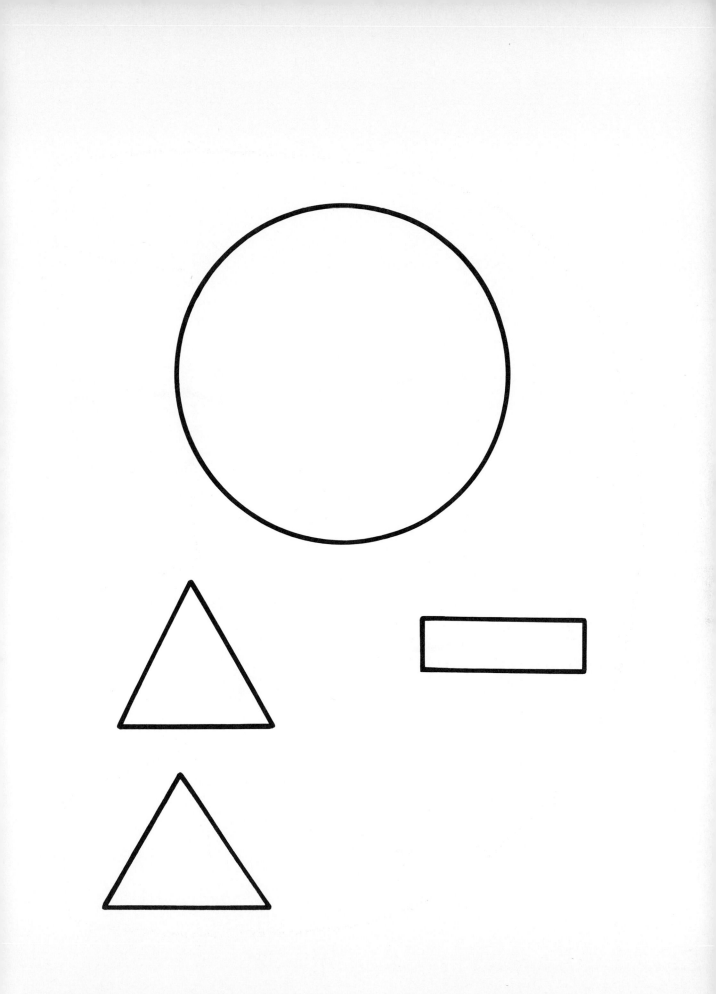

Multisensory letter project: pig (head, ears, tail) 183

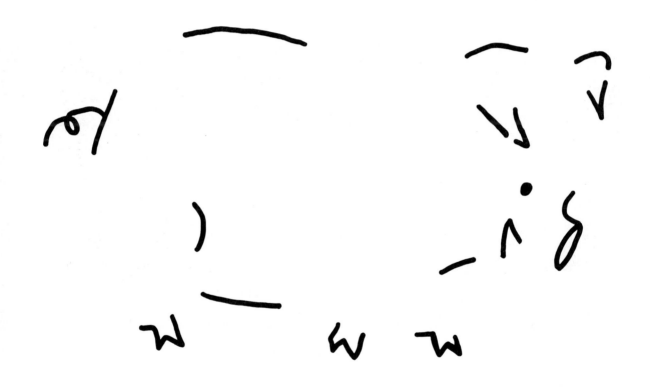

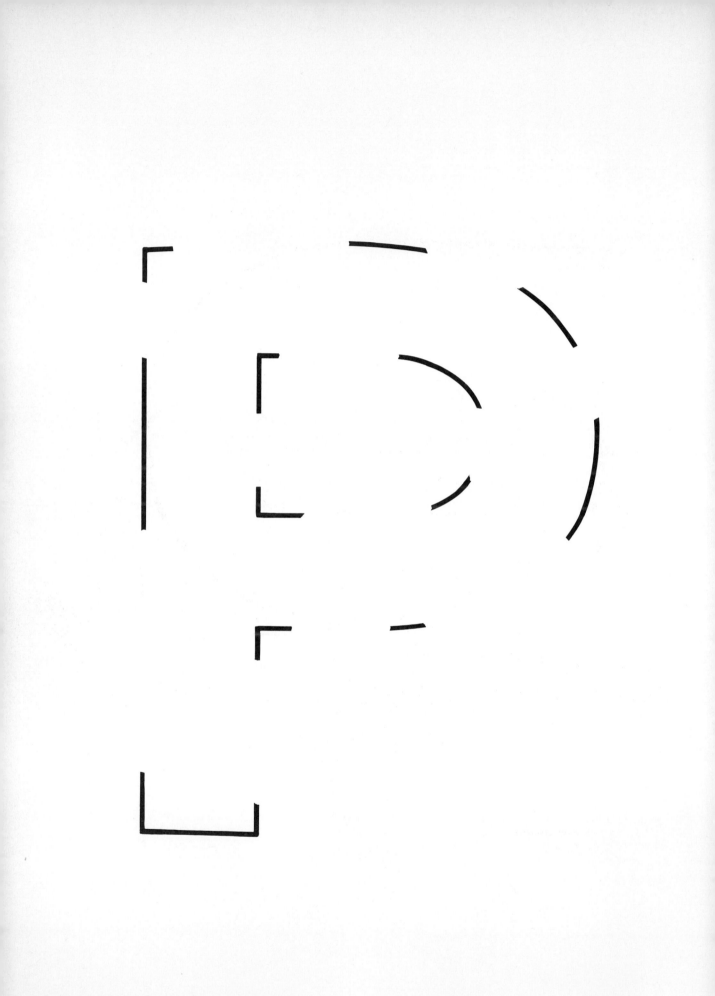

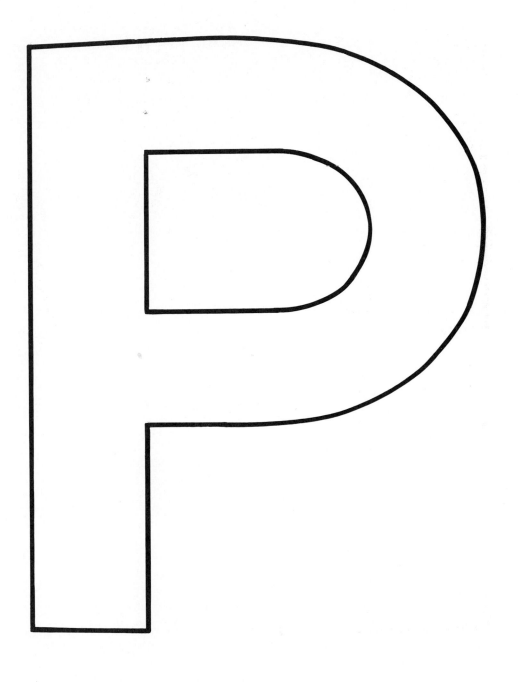

Q q

Letter bag items

quail	question
quart	quill
quarter	quilt
quartz	quince
queen	quiz

Multisensory letter projects

queen (See pattern, pages 193–194.)

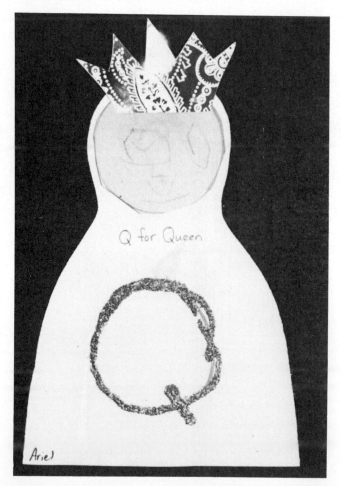

Queen Letter Project

quilt

- Have children use wallpaper samples to make patchwork quilts.

Quilt Letter Project

Other projects

write with quills

queens' crowns

paper quilt

- Draw lines to divide a sheet of paper into four columns and four rows. In the top row place a circle, square, triangle, and rectangle, each of a different color. Ask children to finish the patterns by pasting the appropriate shapes on their quilts.

quilt

- Have children decorate squares of fabric with markers. (Or have children dip a hand in paint and make a handprint on a fabric square.) Sew squares together and quilt or tie with yarn.

The class made a quilt for the wall.

Thinking skills

Comprehension:

- Have children respond to questions such as those in *This Can Lick a Lollipop.*

- Discuss with children the concepts quiet/loud, quick/slow.

- Let children explore a set of quilt pieces (possibly wallpaper samples). Have them compare, contrast, and describe the shapes.

- Use visual closure cards. (See examples, pages 195–198.)

Memory:

- Designate a "magic" page in books that are read.

- Use the memory book with a variety of simple quilt patterns.

Decision making:

- Ask children to match quilt pieces that are alike.

- Have children list places where they need to be quiet and places where they can be loud.

Creativity:

- Have children brainstorm things that are quick or things that are quiet.

- Let children act out the fable of the hare and the tortoise, depicting the concept quick/slow.

Food projects

quiche Lorraine (*Cook and Learn*)
zucchini quiche (*Cook and Learn*)

Books

Q Is for Duck: An Alphabet Guessing Game, by Mary Eltings and Michael Folsom, illustrated by Jack Kent. New York: Clarion Books, 1980.

The Quarreling Book, by Charlotte Zolotow, illustrated by Arnold Lobel. New York: Harper & Row, 1963.

The Queen Wanted to Dance, by Mercer Mayer. New York: Simon and Schuster, 1971.

The Quicksand Book, by Tomie de Paola. New York: Holiday House, 1977.

The Quiet Noisy Book, by Margaret Wise Brown, illustrated by Leonard Weisgard. New York: Harper & Row, 1950.

Quiet! There's a Canary in the Library, by Don Freeman. San Carlos, Calif.: Golden Gate Children's Books, 1969.

Quilts in the Attic, by Robbin Fleisher, illustrated by Ati Forberg. New York: Macmillan, 1978.

This Can Lick a Lollipop, English words by Joel Rothman, Spanish words by Argentina Palacios, photographs by Patricia Ruben. Garden City, N.Y.: Doubleday, 1979.

Songs and fingerplays

Queen of Hearts

Science projects

Set up a question box.

- Have children dictate or write questions about items from nature. Choose two per day to answer.

Field trips and visitors

quarry
quilt shop
quilter
quartet

Queens arrived at school all week.

Multisensory letter project: queen (body) 193

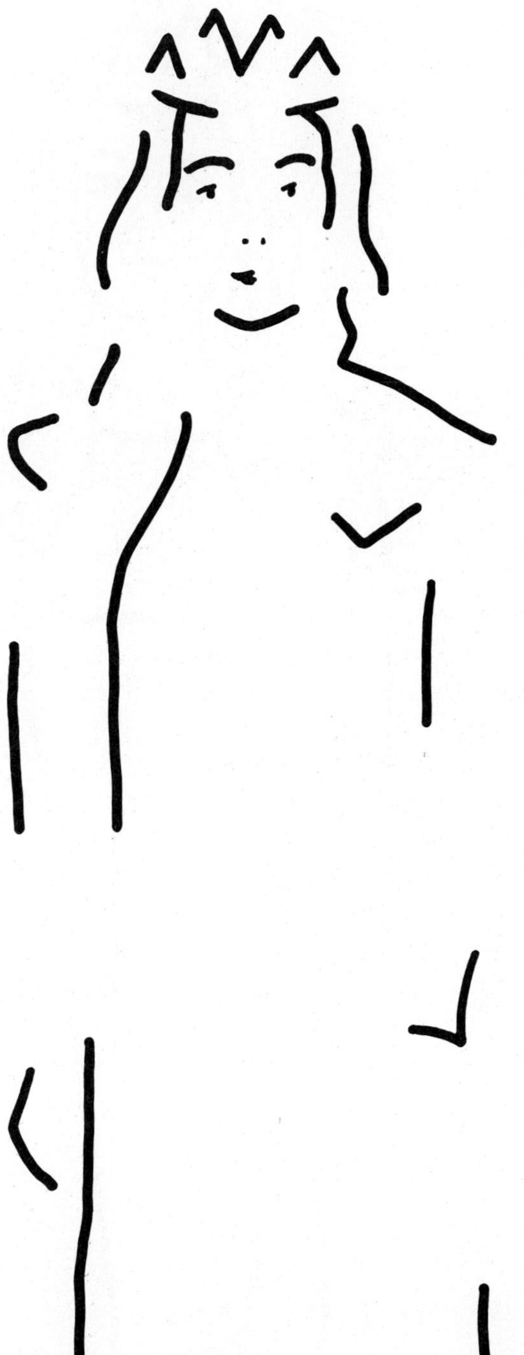

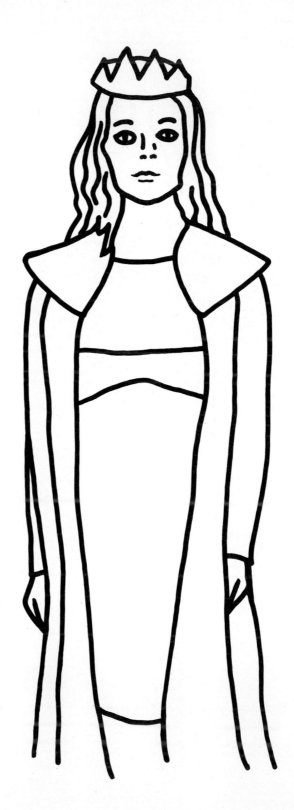

196 Visual closure card: queen

Rr

rabbit (See pattern, page 204.)

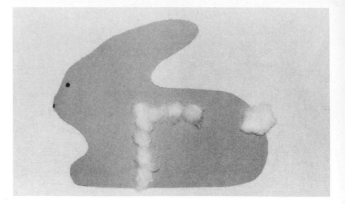

Rabbit Letter Project

Letter bag items

rabbit	ribbon
radish	ring
rainbow	rock
raisin	roller skate
rake	rope
rattle	rubber band
recorder	ruler
red	

Multisensory letter projects

robot (See pattern, page 203.)

Robot Letter Project

Other projects

rainbows

- To help children place the colors appropriately, put red, orange, yellow, green, blue, indigo, and violet paint from left to right in the sections of an egg carton.

rock painting

rockets

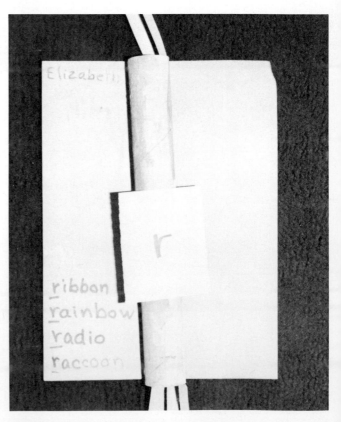

Rocket Project

recipes

- Have children dictate or write their own recipes.

rattles

rhythm instruments

ribbon collage

rectangle collage

round collage (use lids, tubes, split peas, etc.)

red collage

recycling papers, cans, or bottles

Thinking skills

Comprehension:

- Let children tell rhymes and/or riddles.
- Ask children to listen to various rhythms and describe similarities and differences.
- Provide one of the following sets for children to explore: rocks, reptiles, rings, ribbons, or ropes. Have them touch, look at, and describe each item.
- Discuss the concept real/pretend.
- Use visual closure cards. (See examples, pages 205–208.)

Memory:

- Let children play *Concentration* using cards made with reptile stickers.
- Use the memory tray with items from the letter bag.
- Use the memory book with pictures of red things.
- Designate "magic" pages in books that are read.

Decision making:

- Have children list things that would fit through a ring.
- Have children classify one of the following sets: rocks, reptiles, rings, ribbons, or ropes. Discuss the classifications.
- Have children classify rhythms. Discuss the classifications.
- Start rock collections. Explain the "rule" governing each collection.

- Let children match rocks to shapes drawn on paper.
- Have children classify items according to whether or not they are usually found in the refrigerator.

Creativity:

- Let children act out *Little Red Riding Hood.*
- Have children brainstorm things that are round, things that are red, and then things that are round and red.

Food projects

raisin rolls
raisins
hot rice salad (*Cook and Learn*)
rice

Books

Applebaums Have a Robot! by Jane Thayer, illustrated by Bari Weissman. New York: William Morrow, 1980.

The Compost Heap, by Harlow Rockwell. Garden City, New York: Doubleday, 1974.

Everybody Needs A Rock, by Byrd Baylor, illustrated by Peter Parnall. New York: Charles Scribner's Sons, 1974.

How Far Will a Rubber Band Stretch? by Mike Thaler, illustrated by Jerry Joyner. New York: Parents Magazine Press, 1974.

Little Rabbit's Loose Tooth, by Lucy Bate, illustrated by Diane de Groat. New York: Scholastic Inc., 1975.

Little Red Riding Hood, told by Mabel Watts, illustrated by Les Gray. Racine, Wis.: Golden Press, 1979.

No Roses for Harry! by Gene Zion, illustrated by Margaret Bloy Graham. New York: Harper & Row, 1958.

The Rabbit, by John Burningham. New York: Thomas Y. Crowell, 1974.

Rain, by Robert Kalan, illustrated by Donald Crews. New York: Greenwillow Books, 1978.

Rain Rain Rivers, by Uri Shulevitz. New York: Farrar, Straus, & Giroux, 1969.

Roland: The Minstrel Pig, by William Steig. New York: Windmill Books and E. P. Dutton, 1968.

Roses Are Red. Are Violets Blue?? by Alice and Martin Provensen. New York: Random House, 1973.

Rosie's Walk, by Pat Hutchins. New York: Macmillan, 1968.

Round Robin, by Jack Kent. Englewood Cliffs, N.J.: Prentice-Hall, 1982.

Songs and fingerplays

Ring Around the Rosy

Five Little Rabbits
Five little rabbits under a log!
  (Hold up a hand.)
This one said, ''I hear a dog!''
  (Hold up thumb.)
This one said, ''I see a man!''
  (Hold up index finger.)
This one said, ''Run while you can!''
  (Hold up middle finger.)
This one said, ''I'm not afraid!''
  (Hold up little ring finger.)
This one said, ''Let's hide in the shade!''
  (Hold up little finger.)
A man and a dog went hurrying by,
And you should have seen those rabbits fly!
  (Put hand quickly behind back.)
                      –Author unknown–

It's Raining
It's raining, it's pouring,
The old man is snoring.
He went to bed and he bumped his head,
And couldn't get up in the morning.
                      –Author unknown–

Science projects

Plant radishes.
Study reptiles.
Observe and learn about roots.
Observe ripples on water.
Study rock formations.
Make a compost heap to recycle organic material.
(See *The Compost Heap.*)

Field trips and visitors

restaurant
roller rink
recycling center
radio announcer

Children visited a restaurant and played restaurant when they returned to the classroom.

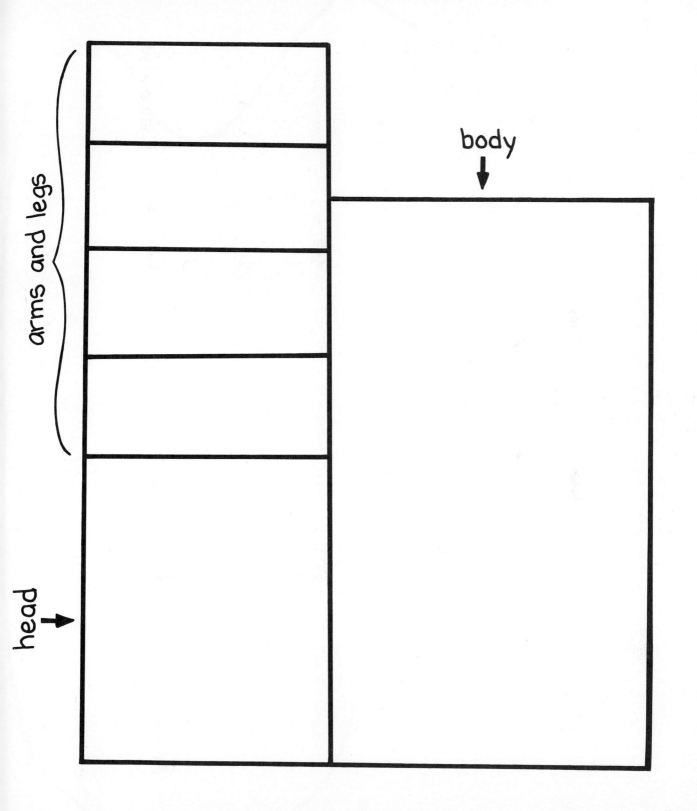

arms and legs

body

head

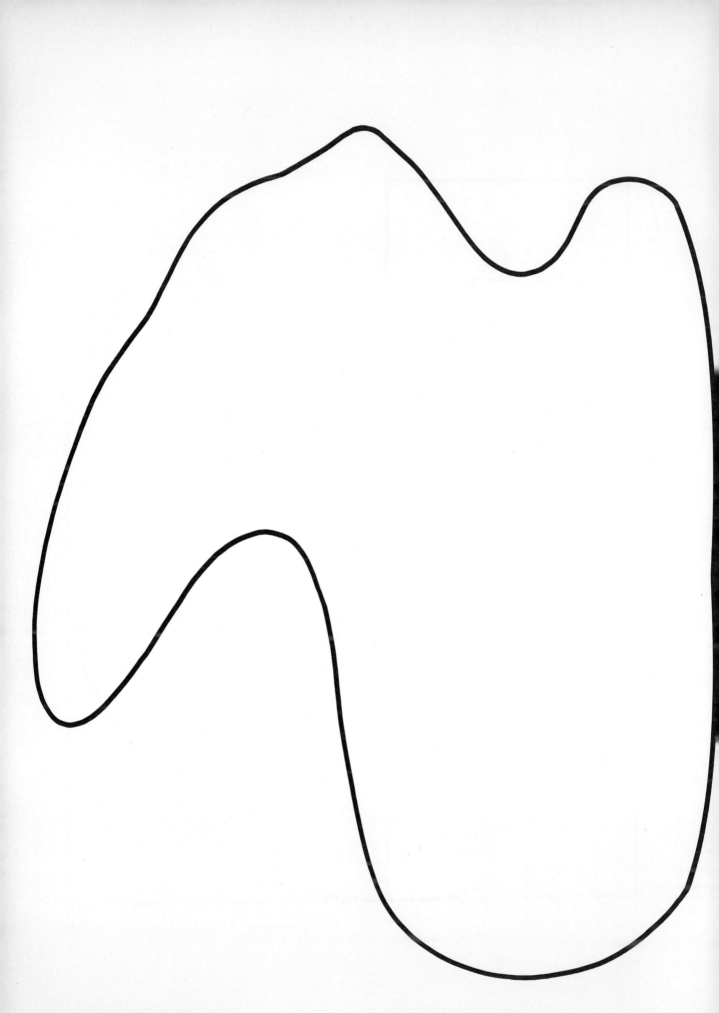

206 Visual closure card: rocking horse

208 Visual closure card: *R*/Golden letter

S

S s

Letter bag items

sandwich	sponge
satellite	spoon
scissors	squid
skate	stamp
slipper	star
soap	starfish
sock	stop sign
spider	

Multisensory letter projects

sun (See pattern, page 213.)

■ Show children how to attach tissue paper rays to sun with liquid starch.

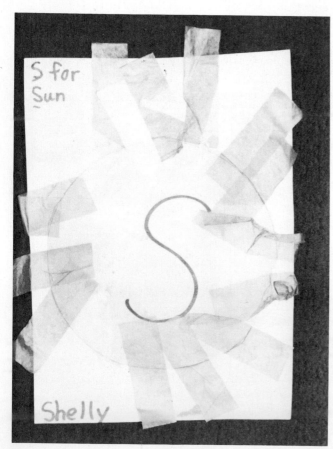

Sun Letter Project

spider (See pattern, page 214.)

■ Have children attach eight legs to be accurate.

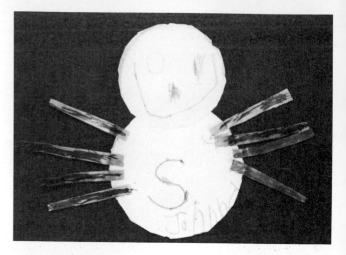

Spider Letter Project

Other projects

sponge printing

Superman S (yellow S on red background)

sand painting

■ Mix dry sand and dry paint. Have children make a pattern with glue. Shake sand/paint mixture on glue and remove excess.

silvery collage

square collage

sequin collage

sewing

space ships

■ Paint paper towel roll. Help children glue it to a sheet of paper. Have them add a paper flame at the base of the space ship.

scissor snipping

Thinking skills

Comprehension:

■ Study safety.

■ Discuss with children the concepts of smooth/rough, short/tall, soft/hard, stop/start.

■ Help children learn what street signs mean.

- Provide one of the following sets for children to explore: spoons, shoes, socks, soaps, or stones. Have them touch, look at, and describe each item.
- Use visual closure cards. (See examples, pages 215–218.)
- Have children explore sizes, shapes, and textures of different kinds of seeds.

Memory:

- Ask children to take off their shoes and put them in the middle of a circle. Then have them try to match pairs of shoes with the correct person.
- Use the memory tray with items from the letter bag.
- Use the memory book with pictures of square things.
- Designate a "magic" page in books that are read.

Decision making:

- Have children sort objects according to whether they are smooth/rough or soft/hard.
- Have children classify one of the following sets: spoons, shoes, socks, soaps or stones. Discuss the classifications.
- Have children arrange seeds from smallest to largest.
- Read *Small Worlds Close Up.* Have children try to figure out the subjects of the photographs.

Creativity:

- Have children brainstorm things that can be seen or square things.
- Have children dictate or write a story about a seed that grew and grew.

Food projects

salad (*Cook and Learn*)
salad bar
soup (*Cook and Learn*)
sandwich (*Cook and Learn*)
stone soup
snow cones

Books

The Berenstain Bears and the Sitter, by Stan and Jan Berenstain. New York: Random House, 1981.

The Carrot Seed, by Ruth Krauss, illustrated by Crockett Johnson. New York: Scholastic Inc., 1945.

How a Seed Grows, by Helene J. Jordan, illustrated by Joseph Low. New York: Thomas Y. Crowell, 1960.

My Snail, by Herbert H. Wong and Matthew F. Vessel, illustrated by Jean Day Zallinger. Reading, Mass.: Addison-Wesley, 1976.

One Snail and Me, by Emilie W. McLeod, illustrated by Walter Lorraine. Boston: Little, Brown and Company, 1961.

The Plant Sitter, by Gene Zion, illustrated by Margaret Bloy Graham. New York: Harper & Row, 1959.

Small Worlds Close Up, by Lisa Grillone and Joseph Gennaro. New York: Crown, 1978.

Snail, Where Are You? by Tomi Ungerer. New York: Harper & Row, 1962.

Spot's First Walk, by Eric Hill. New York: G. P. Putnam's Sons, 1981.

The Stickleback, by Sacha van Dulm and Jan Riem. Woodbury, N.Y.: Barron's, 1979.

Stone Soup, by Marcia Brown. New York: Charles Scribner's Sons, 1947.

Squiggly Wiggly's Surprise, by Arnold Shapiro, illustrated by Charles Murphy. Los Angeles: Intervisual, 1978.

Summer Is . . . , by Charlotte Zolotow, illustrated by Ruth Lercher Bornstein. New York: Thomas Y. Crowell, 1967.

Swimmy, by Leo Lionni. New York: Pantheon, 1968.

This Can Lick a Lollipop: Body Riddles for Kids, by Joel Rothman and Argentina Palacios, photographs by Patricia Ruben. Garden City, N.Y.: Doubleday, 1979.

Where's Spot? by Eric Hill. New York: G. P. Putnam's Sons, 1980.

Songs and fingerplays

Safety
Stop on the red.
Go on the green.
Get ready yellow
Comes in between.

–Author unknown–

Eensy-Weensy Spider
The eensy-weensy spider
Went up the water spout.
  *(Put index fingers to thumbs to make spider
  climb.)*
Down came the rain
And washed the spider out.
  (Swish hands downward.)
Out came the sun
And dried up all the rain.
  (Have hands meet above head.)
And the eensy-weensy spider
Went up the spout again.
  (Make spider climb again.)

–Author unknown–

Sing a Song of Sixpence

Skip to My Lou

Science projects

Grow sprouts. (See *Cook and Learn.*)
Sprout seeds.
Study spiders.
Make soap.

Field trips and visitors

supermarket
science museum
secretary
stamp collector

Children cheered their entries in a snail race.

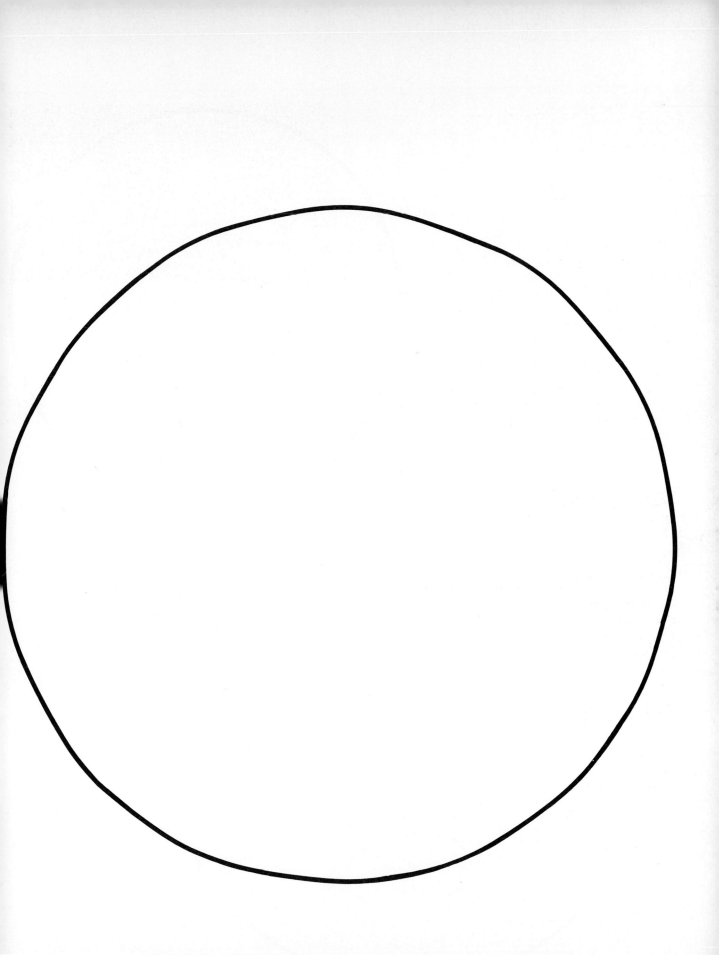

Multisensory letter project: sun 213

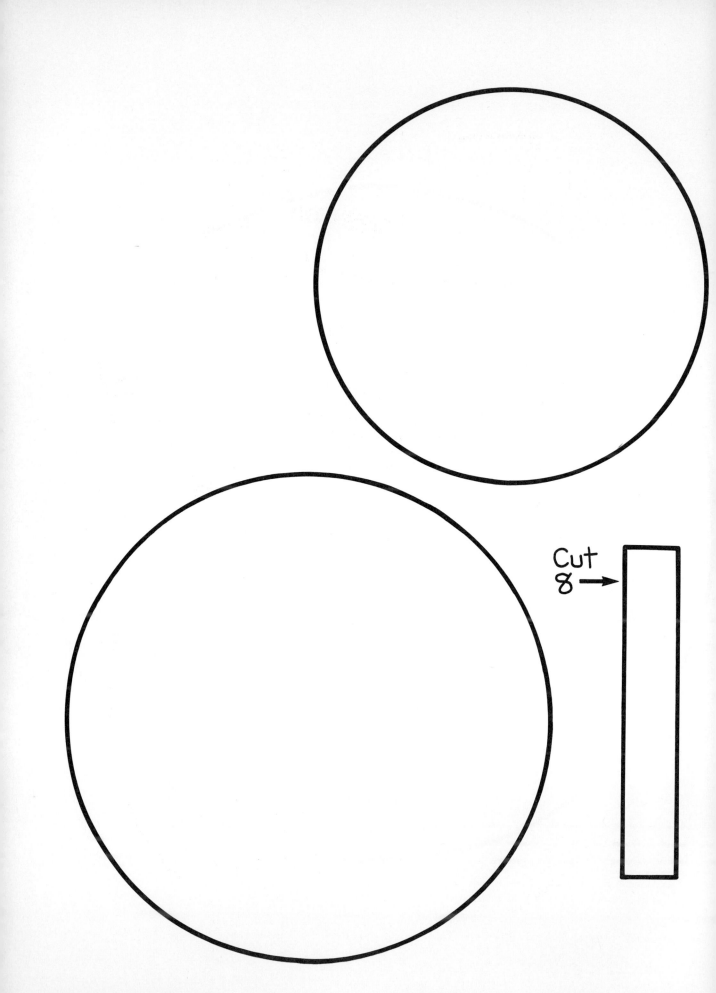

Cut
8 →

216 Visual closure card: snowman

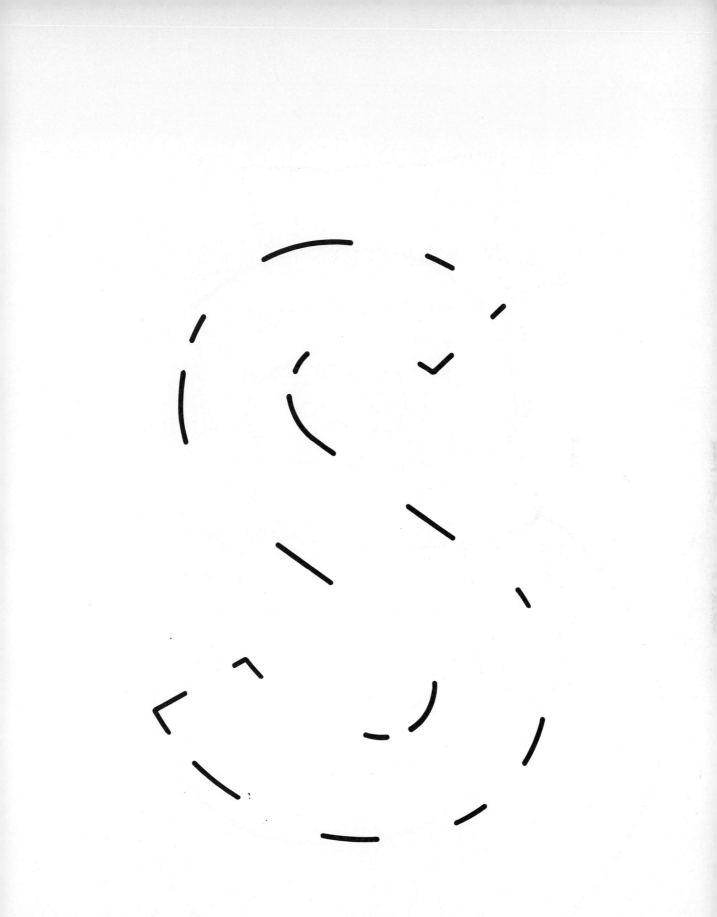

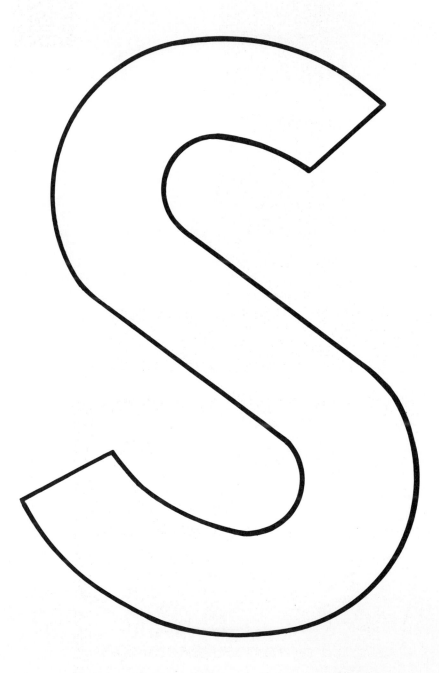

218 Visual closure card: *S*/Golden letter

T

t

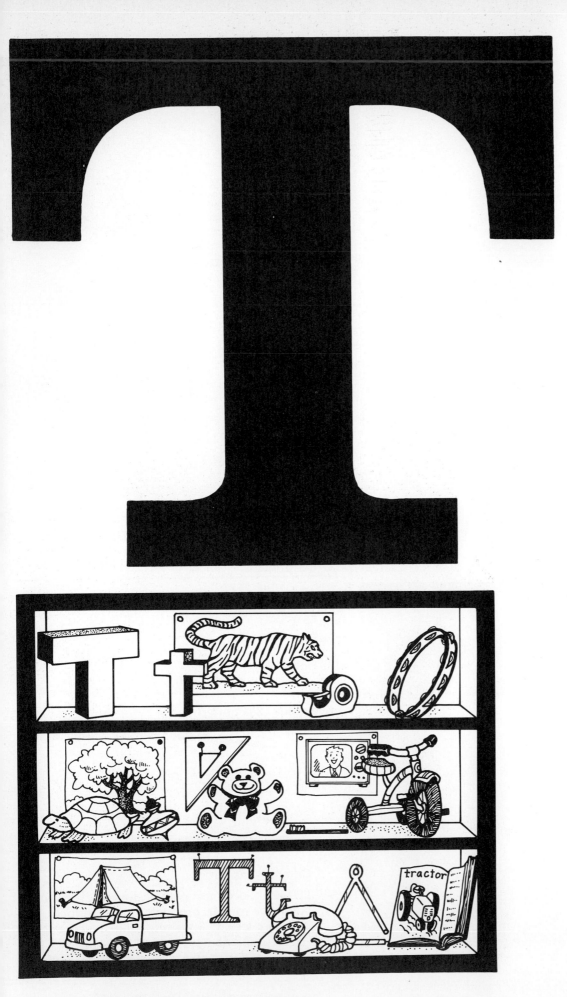

T t

Letter bag items

tambourine	toothbrush
tape	top
telephone	tortilla
tent	tractor
ticket	triangle
tiger	troll
tire	truck
toad	turtle

Multisensory letter projects

tooth (See pattern, page 223.)

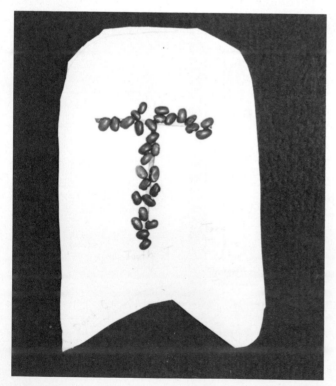

Tooth Letter Project

turtle (See pattern, page 224.)

Turtle Letter Project

Other projects

triangle collage
toothpick collage

tissue collage

top

- Put a pencil through a cardboard circle.

telephone (See pattern, page 225.)

- Write name and phone number on telephone.

tracing

T-shirt designs

Thinking skills

Comprehension:

- Have children taste, smell, look at, feel, and describe tomato products—juice, fresh, canned, stewed, ketchup, aspic, sauce, and paste—on a tomato tasting tray. Discuss the different tastes and textures.

220

- Discuss the concept top/bottom with children.
- Tape record children's voices and play the tape back.
- Use visual closure cards. (See examples, pages 226–229.)
- Have children explore one of the following sets: teddy bears, toothpicks, tees (golf), toys, and teeth. Have them touch, look at, and describe each item.

Memory:

- Use the memory book with pictures of toys.
- Use the memory tray with items from the letter bag.
- Designate a "magic" page in books that are read.

Decision making:

- Have children arrange teddy bears from smallest to largest.
- Have children classify one of the following sets: toothpicks, tees, toys or teeth. Discuss the classifications.
- Have children classify animals as being tame or wild.

Creativity:

- Have children brainstorm animals with tails.
- Ask children to pretend they are toys and show what the toys can do.
- Have children dictate or write a story about a toy that comes to life.

Food projects

tacos (*Cook and Learn*)
tortillas (*Cook and Learn*)
tomato ketchup (*Cook and Learn*)
tofu burgers (*Cook and Learn*)
trail mix (*Cook and Learn*)

Books

The Bear's Toothache, by David McPhail. New York: Penguin Books, 1972.

The Everyday Train, by Amy Ehrlich, illustrated by Martha Alexander. New York: Dial, 1977.

Tikki Tikki Tembo, retold by Arlene Mosel, illustrated by Blair Lent. New York: Scholastic Inc., 1968.

The Train, by David McPhail. Boston: Little, Brown and Company, 1977.

A Treeful of Pigs, by Arnold Lobel, illustrated by Anita Lobel. New York: Scholastic Inc., 1979.

A Tree Is Nice, by Janice May Udry, illustrated by Marc Simont. New York: Harper & Row, 1956.

The Truck Book, by Robert L. Wolfe. Minneapolis: Carolrhoda Books, 1981.

Songs and fingerplays

Ten Little Indians

Twinkle, Twinkle Little Star

*Little Turtle**
There was a little turtle
  (Make fist.)
He lived in a box.
  (Use hands for box.)
He swam in a puddle.
  (Make swimming motion.)
And he climbed on the rocks.
  (Make climbing motion.)
He snapped at a mosquito,
  (Make grabbing motion.)
He snapped at a flea,
  (Make grabbing motion.)
He snapped at a minnow.
  (Make grabbing motion.)
And he snapped at me.
  (Make grabbing motion.)
He caught the mosquito,
  (Clap.)
He caught the flea,
  (Clap.)
He caught the minnow.
  (Clap.)
But he didn't catch me.
  (Shake head and point to self.)

–*Vachel Lindsay*–

*"Little Turtle" reprinted with permission of Macmillan Publishing Company from *Collected Poems* by Vachel Lindsay. Copyright © 1920 by Macmillan Publishing Company, renewed 1948 by Elizabeth C. Lindsay.

I'm a Little Teapot
I'm a little teapot
Short and stout.
Here is my handle.
  (Crook arm and put hand on hip.)
Here is my spout.
  (Extend other arm.)
When I get all steamed up
Hear me shout.
"Just tip me over
And pour me out!"
  (Bend over, as if pouring.)

–*Author unknown*–

Science projects

Make terrariums.
Examine teeth of wild and tame animals.

Field trips and visitors

tailor
telephone company
telephone repair person

Additional ideas

Have a tea party with formal settings.
Play tag.

Children gained new perspectives on trees.

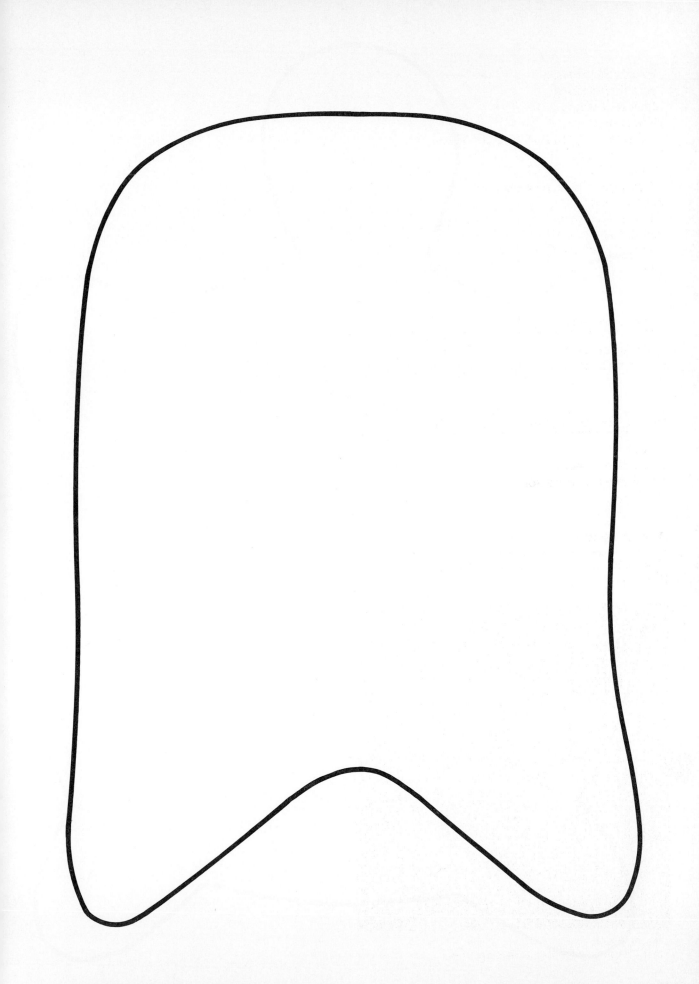

Multisensory letter project: tooth 223

Visual closure card: turtle 227

Visual closure card: *T*/Golden letter 229

U u

umbrella (See pattern, pages 236–237.)

Umbrella Letter Project

Letter bag items*

ukelele	underwear
umbrella	unicorn
under	uniform
umpire	upholstery
undershirt	up

Multisensory letter projects

underwear (See pattern, page 235.)

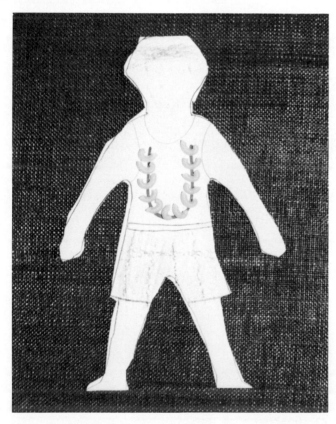

Underwear Letter Project

Other projects

Officer Ugg (See pattern, pages 238–239.)

Officer Ugg Project

*When vowels are introduced, the short sound is emphasized, but we discuss with the children that letters often have more than one sound.

undershirts

- Use brown grocery sacks. Have children decorate them with crayons. Cut arm holes on sides and neck hole from the bottom of the sack.

Thinking skills

Comprehension:

- Ask children to act out the following concepts: up/down, under/over.

The children showed how high *up* they could climb.

- Help children learn about Officer Ugg and Poison Control Centers.*
- Provide one of the following sets for children to explore: umbrellas or pictures of people in uniforms. Have them describe each item.
- Use visual closure cards. (See examples, pages 240–243.)
- Have children listen to scales going up and down on a piano or xylophone.

*Officer Ugg is a symbol used by the American Association of Poison Control Centers (Rocky Mountain Poison Center, Denver, Colorado).

Memory:

- Use the memory book with all of the pictures placed upside down.
- Designate "magic" pages in books that are read.

Decision making:

- Have children classify items in one of the following sets: umbrellas or pictures of people in uniforms. Discuss the classifications.
- Have children play scales up and down on the piano or xylophone.

Creativity:

- Have children brainstorm unusual things.

Food project

upside-down cake

Books

My Red Umbrella, by Robert Bright. New York: W. Morrow, 1959.

The Ugly Duckling, by Hans Christian Anderson, translated by R. P. Keigwin, illustrated by Adrienne Adams. New York: Scribner, 1965.

Umbrella, by Taro Yashima. New York: The Viking Press, 1958.

Upside-Downers, by Mitsumasa Anno. New York: Walker/Weatherhill, 1971.

Songs and fingerplays

Scales, by Hap Palmer (*The Feel of Music* record, Educational Activities, Inc., Freeport, N.Y., 1974.)

Under the Spreading Chestnut Tree
Under the spreading chestnut tree
  (*Spread arms out; touch chest, head [nut],
  fingers together over head.*)
We were happy as could be
  (*Hug self and rock back and forth.*)
With our banjoes on our knees
  (*Strum banjo; slap knees.*)
Under the spreading chestnut tree.
  (*Repeat first step.*)

  –Author unknown–

Science project

Study things that grow under the ground.

Field trips and visitors

exhibition of uniforms
furniture refinisher (upholsterer)
umpire
someone in a uniform (policeman, nurse, etc.)

236 Multisensory letter project: umbrella   Copyright © 1986 by Addison-Wesley Publishing Company, Inc.

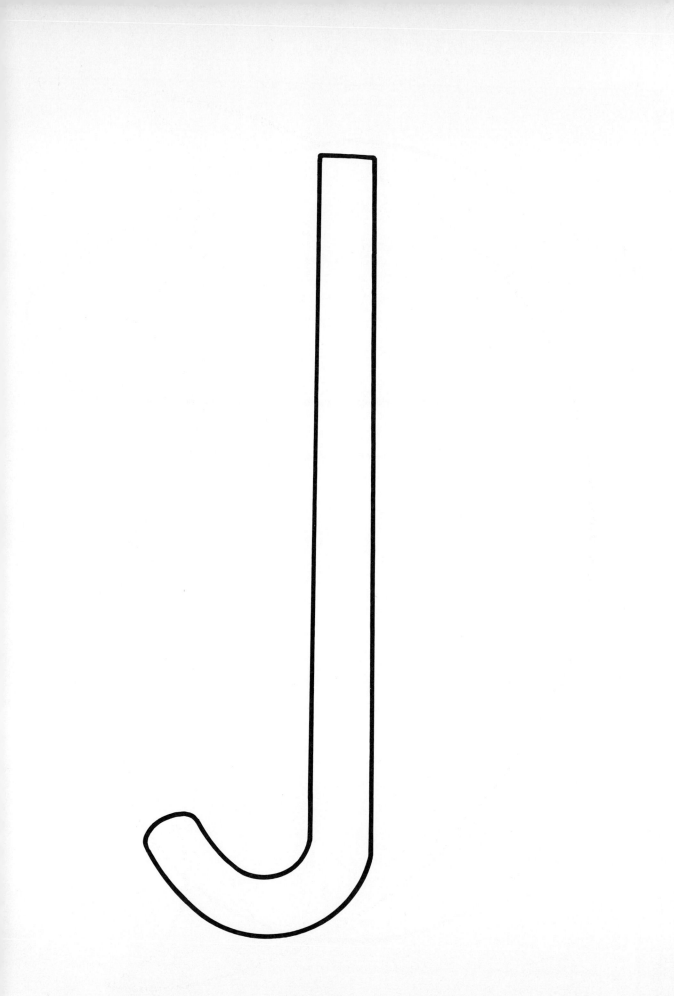

Multisensory letter project: umbrella (handle) 237

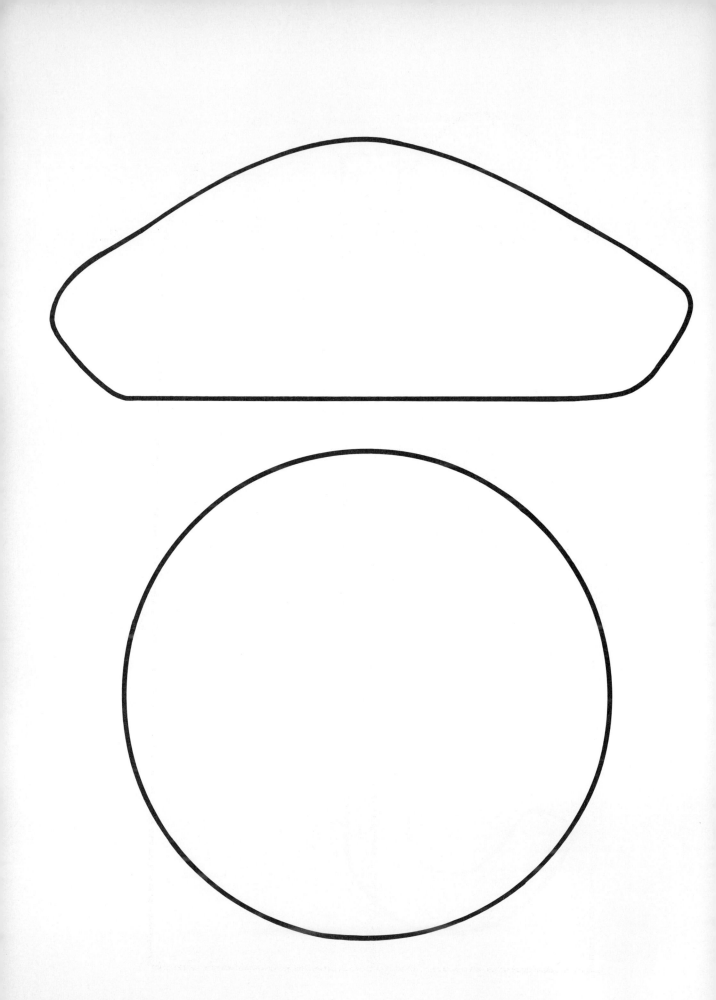

238 Officer Ugg (head, hat)

Visual closure card: umbrella 241

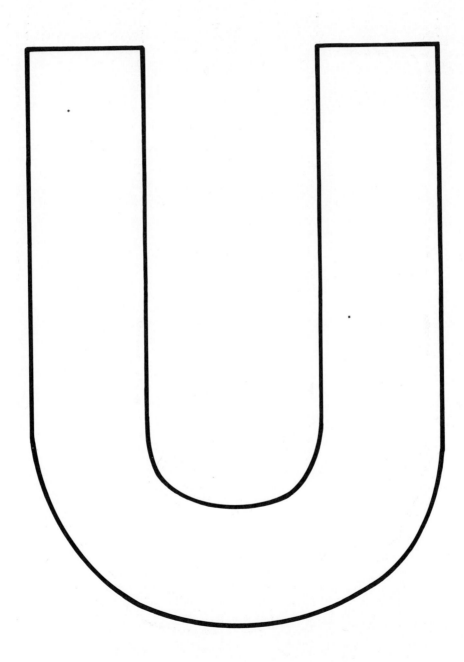

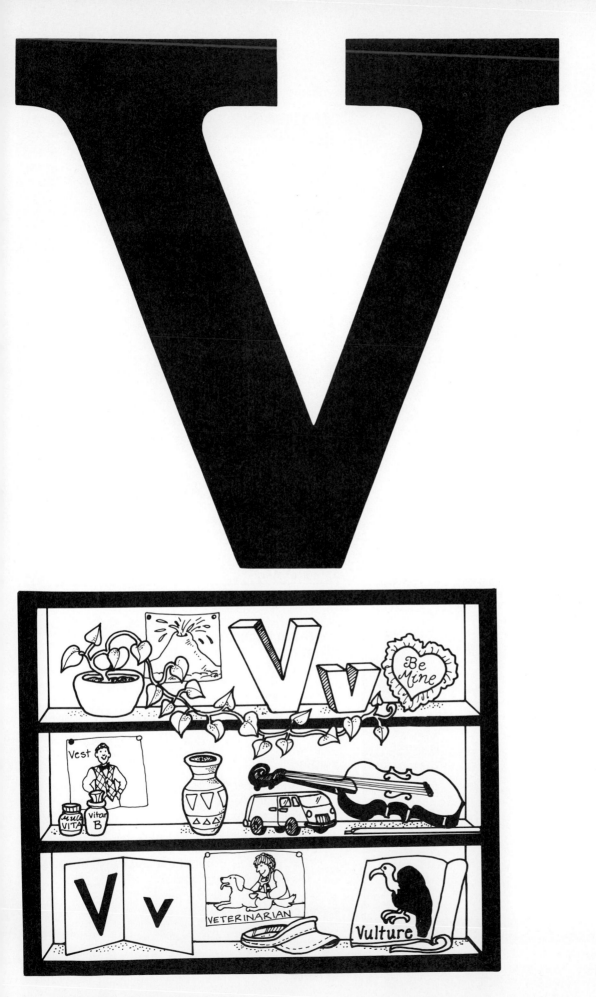

volcano

Volcano Letter Project

Letter bag items

vacuum cleaner	vine
valentine	vinegar
van	violet
vanilla	violin
vase	visor
velvet	volcano
vest	vulture

Multisensory letter projects

vest

Vest Letter Project

Other projects

visors (See pattern, page 249.)

paper cup phones connected with yarn (for vibration)

paper bag vests

violets in vase

- Have children make violets out of purple tissue paper.

volcano

- Mold volcano from papier mache around a glass jar. Paint the outside of the volcano. When ready, the volcano can erupt by following these steps: (1) Mix ¼ C vinegar, ¼ C liquid detergent, and red food coloring in the jar; (2) Add 6 T baking soda that has been dissolved in warm water.

velvet collage

Thinking skills

Comprehension:

- Provide a variety of vegetables on a vegetable tasting tray for children to look at, feel, smell, taste, and describe. Have them compare slices and wholes according to color, texture, shape, etc.
- Show children how to make vibrations using their voices, rubber bands, and other items.
- Use visual closure cards. (See examples, pages 250–253.)
- Use a touch box. Have children put a hand in to discriminate between the feel of velvet and the feel of velcro.
- Have children try to recognize classmates just by listening to their voices.

Memory:

- Use the memory book with pictures of various vehicles.
- Use the memory tray with vehicles.
- Designate a "magic" page in books that are read.

Decision making:

- Have children classify valentines. Discuss the classifications.
- Have children classify vibrations into high and low sounds.
- Have children classify sets of vehicles or vegetables. Discuss the classifications.

Creativity:

- Have children brainstorm types of vehicles or vegetables.
- Have children dictate or write a message to a favorite valentine.

Food projects

vegetable salad (*Cook and Learn*)
raw vegetable tasting
vegetable soup (*Cook and Learn*)
vanilla ice cream (*Cook and Learn*)

Books

A Day in the Life of a Veterinarian, by William Jaspersohn. Boston: Little, Brown and Company, 1978.

The Night Vegetable Eater, by Elke and Ted Musicant, illustrated by Jeni Bassett. New York: Dodd, Mead and Company, 1981.

The Rabbit Is Next, by Gladys Leithauser and Lois Breitmeyer, illustrated by Linda Powell. Racine, Wis.: Golden Press, 1978.

What Can She Be? A Veterinarian, by Gloria and Esther Goldreich, photographs by Robert Ipcar. New York: Lothrop, Lee, and Shepard, 1972.

Science projects

Study things that vibrate.
Study vision.

Field trips and visitors

veterinary hospital
veterinarian
violinist

Children model their visors.

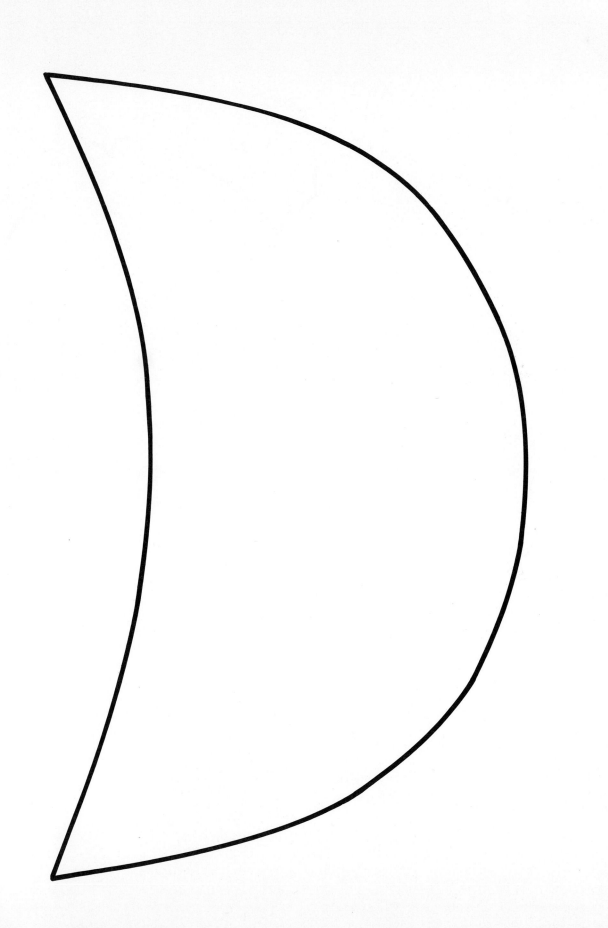

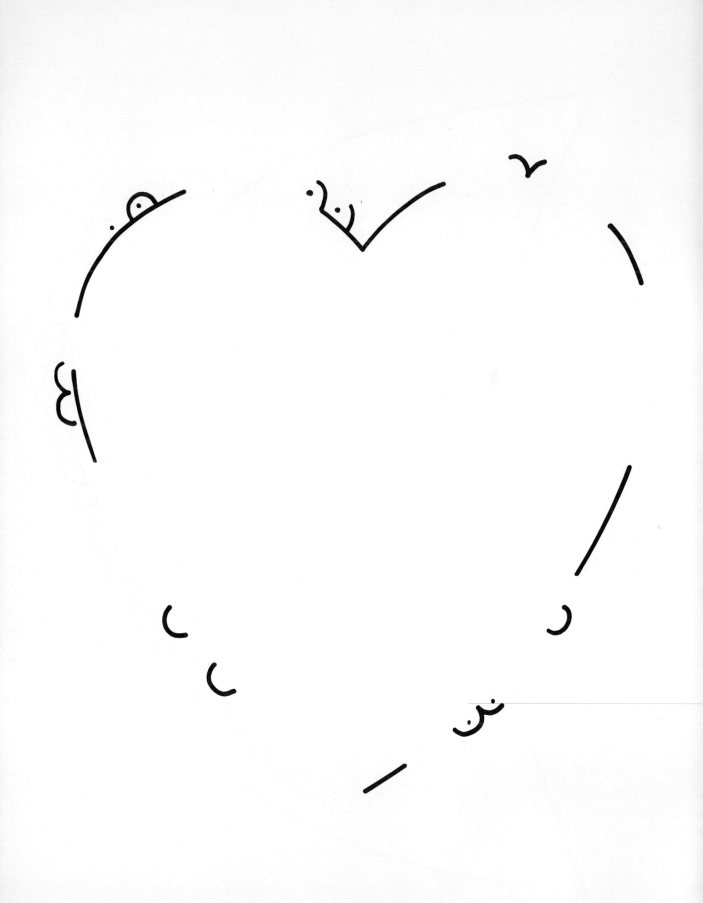

250 Visual closure card: valentine

Visual closure card: valentine 251

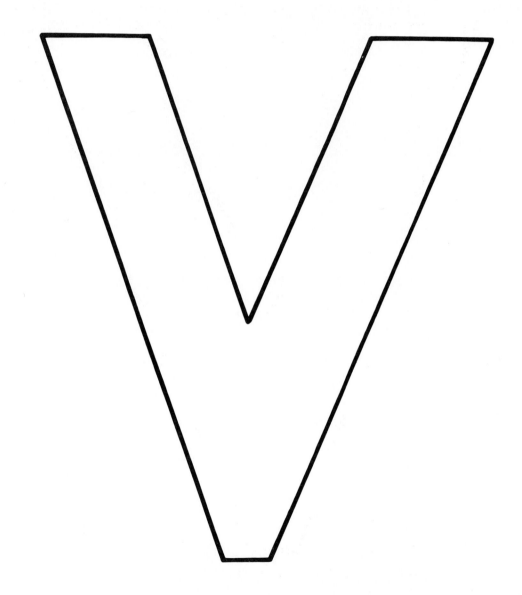

Visual closure card: *V*/Golden letter 253

W

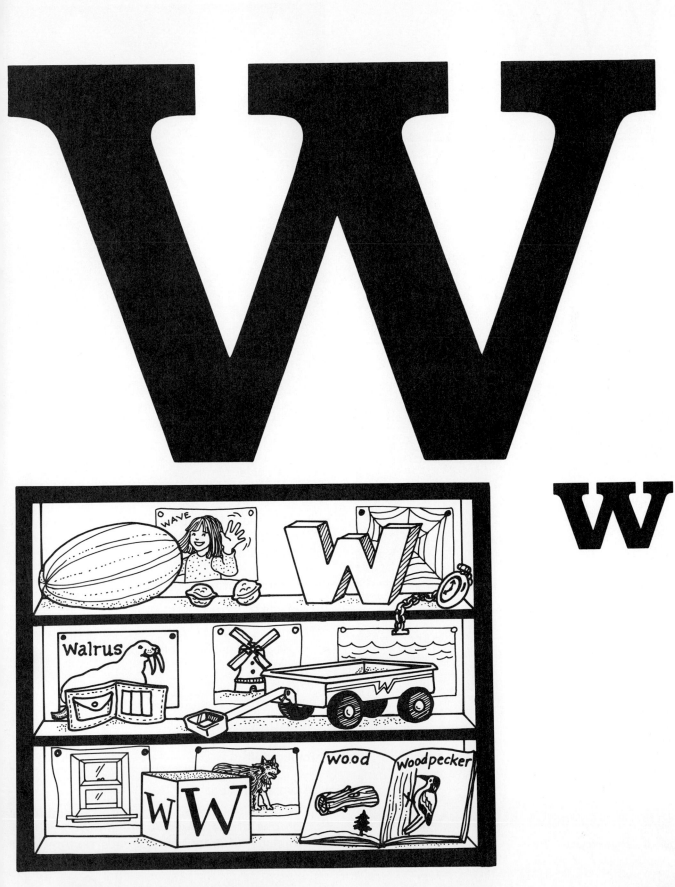

w

Ww

windmill (See pattern, pages 260–261.)

Windmill Letter Project

Letter bag items

waffles	windmill
wagon	window
wall	wing
walnut	witch
walrus	wolf
watch	woman
web	woodpecker
wig	

Multisensory letter projects

witch (See pattern, page 259.)

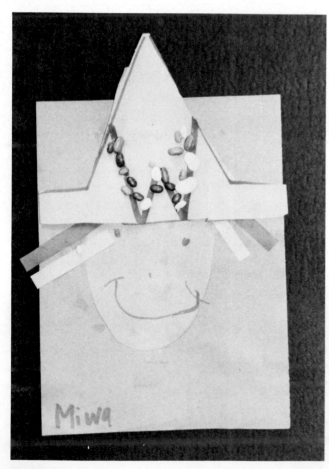

Witch Letter Project

Other projects

wizard hats

■ Have each child make sponge prints on large construction paper. Roll the paper into a pointed hat and staple.

water color painting

wood collage

webs

■ Use white chalk on black paper.

wagons

wings

Thinking skills

Comprehension:

■ Take children on a walk with special emphasis on one of the senses. Ask them to identify as many different sights, sounds, textures, or odors as possible.

- Have children examine walnuts to note differences in size, texture, and color.

- Have children observe objects in water. Pour water from container to container.

- Use visual closure cards. (See examples, pages 262–265.)

- Ask children to describe the weather each day.

Memory:

- Use the memory book with pictures of different windows.

- Designate "magic" pages in books that are read.

Decision making:

- Have children classify walnuts. Discuss the classifications.

- Let children match types of clothing to types of weather.

- Ask children to predict which container holds more water than another. Test their predictions.

- Ask children to predict which objects sink and which float in water. Test their predictions.

- Have children arrange washers in sequence from largest to smallest.

Creativity:

- Ask children to make wishes. These can be dictated or written on clouds and hung if desired.

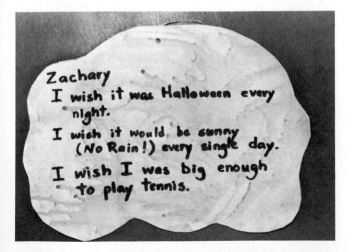

Zachary
I wish it was Halloween every night.
I wish it would be sunny (No Rain!) every single day.
I wish I was big enough to play tennis.

He fingerpainted a cloud and then dictated his wishes.

- Have children brainstorm things that can be seen, heard, felt, or smelled on a walk from school.

- Let children act out *Where the Wild Things Are.*

Food projects

waffles (*Cook and Learn*)
walnuts to shell and taste

Books

Cloudy With a Chance of Meatballs, by Judi Barrett and Ron Barrett. New York: Scholastic Inc., 1978.

Inch by Inch, by Leo Lionni. New York: Astor-Honor, 1960.

The Web in the Grass, by Berniece Freschet, illustrated by Roger Duvoisin. New York: Charles Scribner's Sons, 1972.

When the Wind Stops, by Charlotte Zolotow, illustrated by Joe Lasker. New York: Abeland-Schuman, 1962.

Where the Wild Things Are, by Maurice Sendak. New York: Harper & Row, 1963.

Whistle for Willie, by Ezra Jack Keats. New York: The Viking Press, 1964.

Willaby, by Rachel Isadora. New York: Macmillan, 1977.

William's Doll, by Charlotte Zolotow, illustrated by William Pene DuBois. New York: Harper & Row, 1972.

Wings, by Mary Kennedy, illustrated by Patti Stren. New York: Scholastic Inc., 1980.

Songs and fingerplays

Wee Willie Winkie
Wee Willie Winkie
Runs through the town
Upstairs and downstairs
In his nightgown.
Rapping at the window
Crying through the lock
Is everyone into bed?
It's almost eight o'clock.

–Author unknown–

Days of the Week (Youngheart: *We All Live Together Vol. 4,* Youngheart Records, Los Angeles, 1978)

Science projects

Experiment with weight using walnuts on a balance scale.
Observe the webs of spiders.

Field trips and visitors

weather person
weather station
water plant
waiter

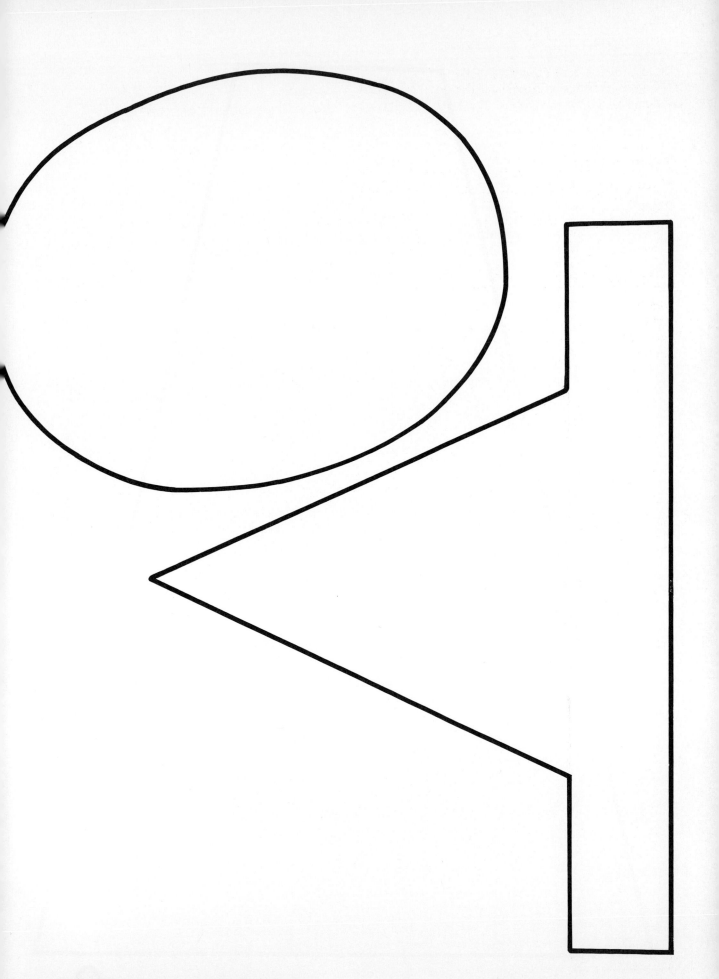

Multisensory letter project: witch 259

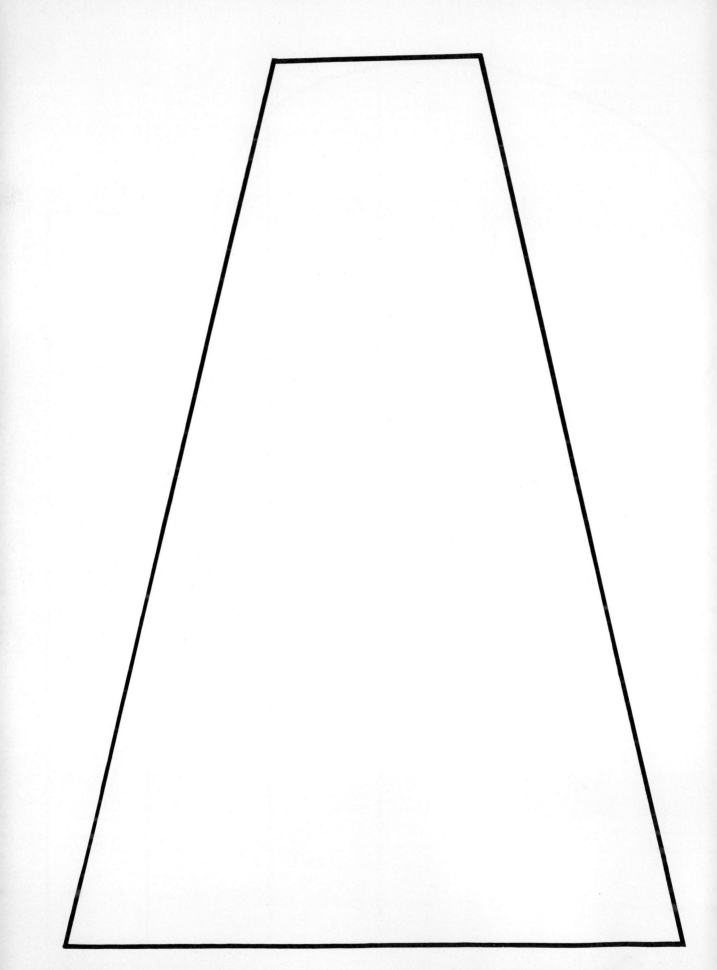

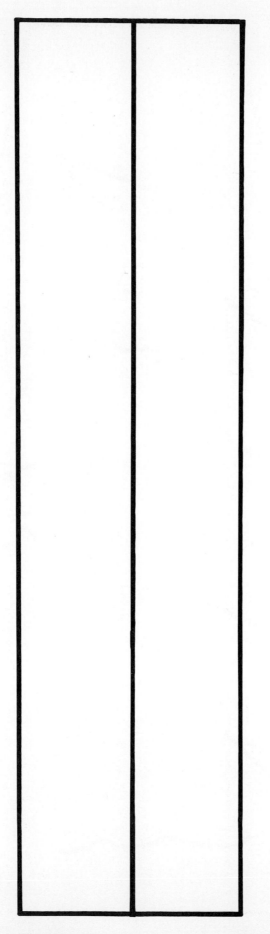

Multisensory letter project: windmill (vanes) 261

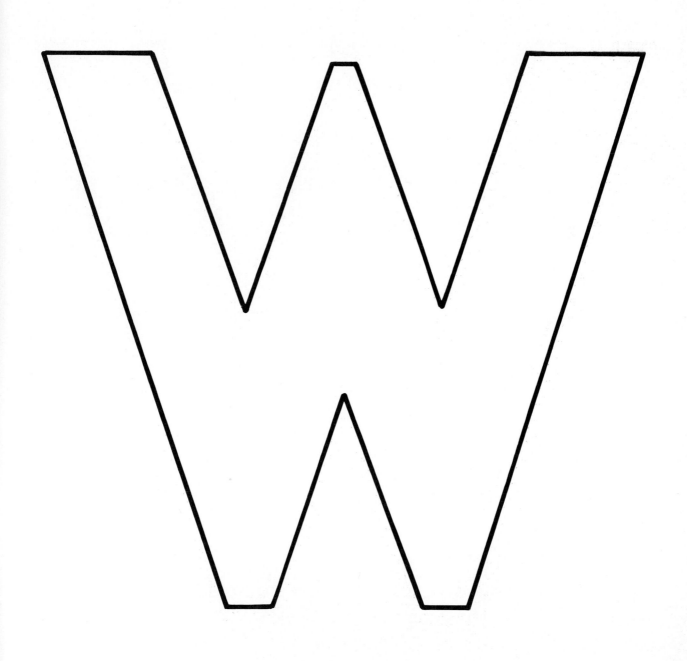

X x

Letter bag items*

ax	mix
box	ox
exercise	six
exit	saxophone
fox	X-ray
lox	

Multisensory letter projects

X-ray

- Use black paper with white lettering.

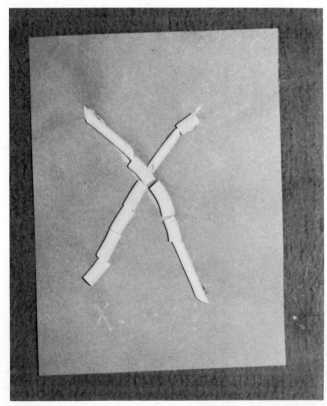

X-ray Letter Project

*We emphasize the "x" sound as heard in words such as *fox.* We also explain the other sounds for *x.*

ax (See pattern for blade, page 271.)

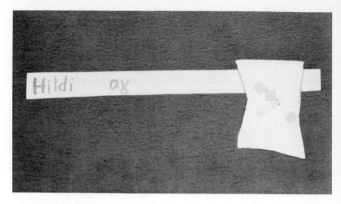

Ax Letter Project

Other projects

box (See pattern, page 272. Cut on solid lines; fold on dots.)

treasure box

- Have children paint egg cartons, then add glitter while the paint is still wet.

Thinking skills

Comprehension:

- Have children examine X-rays. Place film on windows for viewing.

- Provide a set of boxes for children to examine. Have them touch, look at, and describe each one.

- Use visual closure cards (See examples, pages 273–276.)

Memory:

- Use the memory book with pictures of people engaged in various forms of exercise.

- Designate "magic" pages in books that are read.

Decision making:

- Have children find their way through a maze where *X* marks the spot.

- Have children classify boxes. Discuss the classifications.

- Let children match X-rays to pictures of parts of the body.

Creativity:

- Have children brainstorm things that would fit into a given box.
- Let children dictate or write a story about something they might find if they followed a map to where *X* marks the spot.

Food project

Mix fresh fruits or vegetables.

Books

The Box Book, by Cecilia Maloney, illustrated by Carolyn Bracken. Racine, Wis.: Golden Press, 1978.

Christina Katerina and the Box, by Patricia Lee Gauch, illustrated by Doris Burn. New York: Coward, McCann & Geoghegan, 1971.

Little Max, the Cement Mixer, by Renee Bartkowski, illustrated by Robert Doremus. Chicago: Rand McNally, 1975.

The Skeleton Inside You, by Philip Balestrino, illustrated by Don Bolognese. New York: Scholastic Inc., 1971.

Songs and fingerplays

Jack in the Box
Jack in the box
  (Make a fist with thumb on top.)
Sits so-o-o still.
Will he come out?
Yes! He will.
  (Raise thumb quickly.)
Jack in the box
  (Reform fist with thumb on top.)
Sits so-o-o still.
Will he come out?
No! He won't.
  (Shake head.)

—Author unknown—

Science project

Use X-rays to introduce study of the skeleton, various types of joints, etc.

Field trips and visitors

cement mixer at a construction site
saxophonist

Additional ideas

Bury treasure (X marks the spot). Children dress as pirates and follow clues to the treasure.

A pirate checks the bounty after an X-Marks-the-spot treasure hunt.

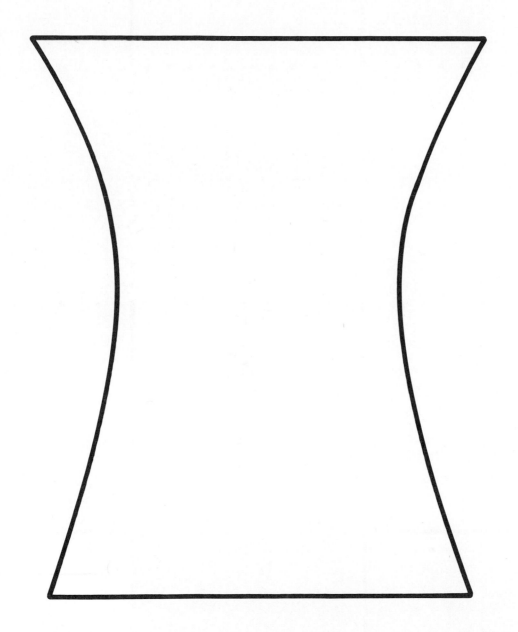

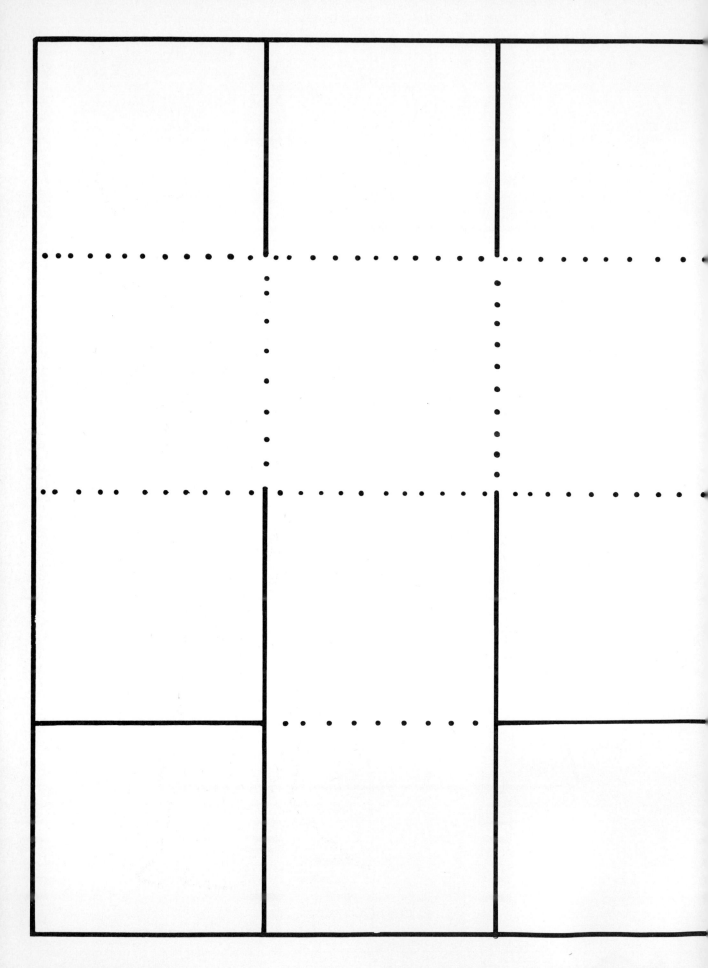

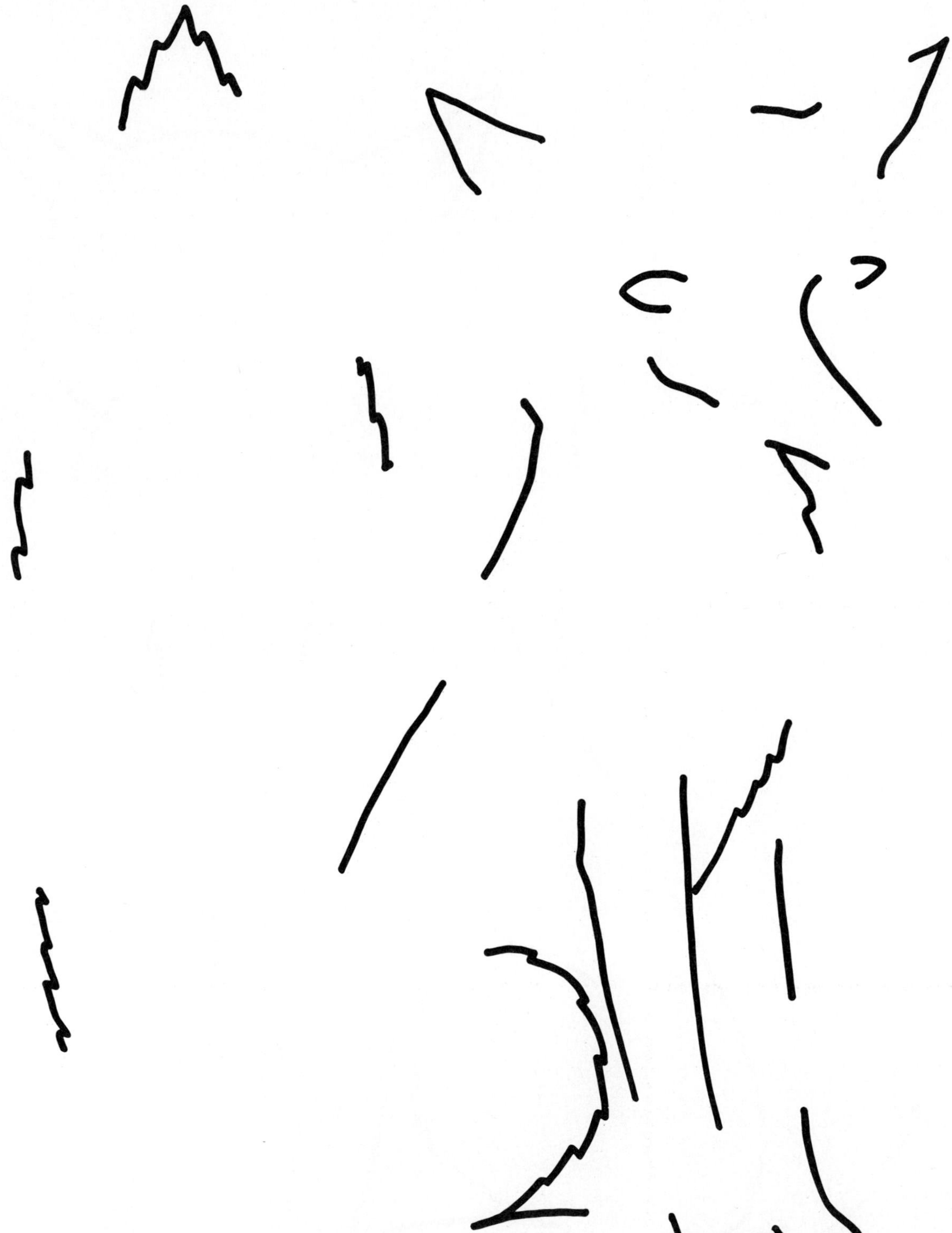

274 Visual closure card: fox

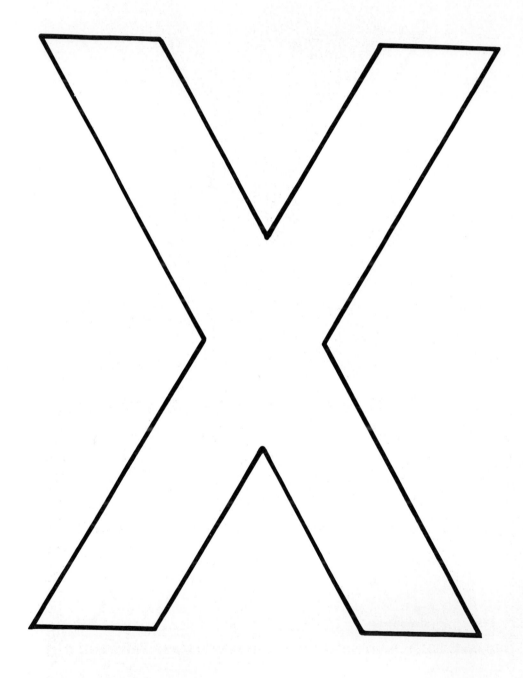

Y y

Y y

Letter bag items

yacht

yak

yam

yard

yardstick

yarn

yeast

yell

yellow

yield sign

yo-yo

yogurt

yolk

Multisensory letter projects

Yellow yarn *Y*

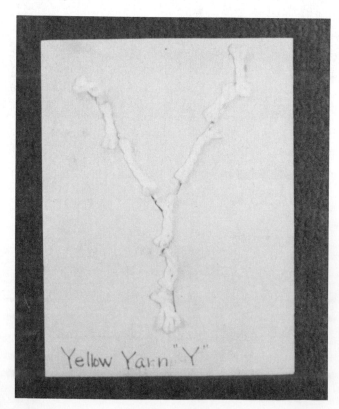

Yellow Yarn *Y* Letter Project

yo-yo (See pattern, page 281.)

■ Use elastic for the string.

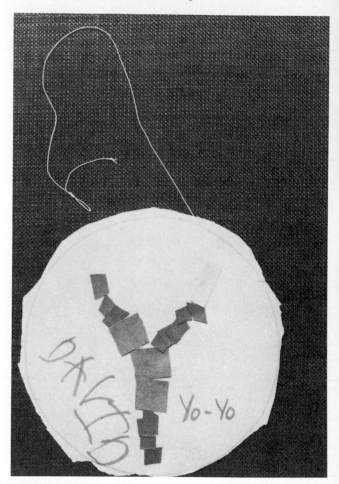

Yo-yo Letter Project

Other projects

yarn sewing on burlap

egg yolk painting

pencil holder

■ Cover a yogurt or frozen orange juice container with glue and have children wrap it with yarn.

yarn thing

■ Have children make something out of a piece of yarn without cutting it.

Thinking skills

Comprehension:

■ Have children measure things with yardsticks.

- Discuss with children the concepts young/old and yesterday/today/tomorrow.
- Have children explore a variety of types of yarn. Ask them to touch, look at, describe, and compare each type.
- Use visual closure cards. (See examples, pages 282–285.)

Memory:
- Use the memory book with pictures of yellow things.
- Designate "magic" pages in books that are read.

Decision making:
- Have children classify different types of yarn. Discuss the classifications.
- Have children compare measurements made with yardsticks.
- Have children classify a collection of yellow objects. Discuss the classifications.

Creativity:
- Have children brainstorm yellow things.

Food projects

yogurt (*Cook and Learn*)
yogurt shakes (*Cook and Learn*)

Books

Little Blue and Little Yellow: A Story for Pippo and Ann and Other Children, by Leo Lionni. New York: I. Obolensky, 1959.

What Does the Rooster Say, Yoshio? by Edith Battles. Chicago: Albert Whitman, 1978.

Yertle the Turtle, and Other Stories, by Dr. Seuss. New York: Random House, 1958.

Songs and fingerplays

Months of the Year, from Youngheart: *We All Live Together, Vol. 2,* Littlehouse Music (ASCAP), Music Education Service, Los Angeles, 1978.

Yankee Doodle

Yellow Rose of Texas

Science projects

Sprout yams.
Experiment with yeast.

Field trips and visitors

yacht harbor
yarn shop
yodeler

The yard provided an exciting painting environment.

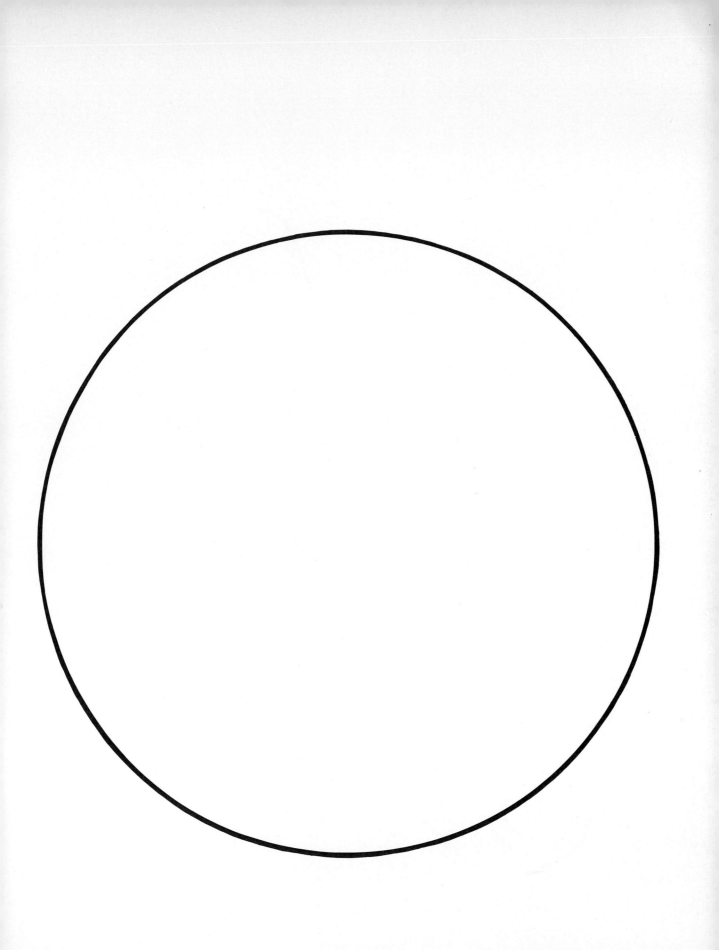

Multisensory letter project: yo-yo 281

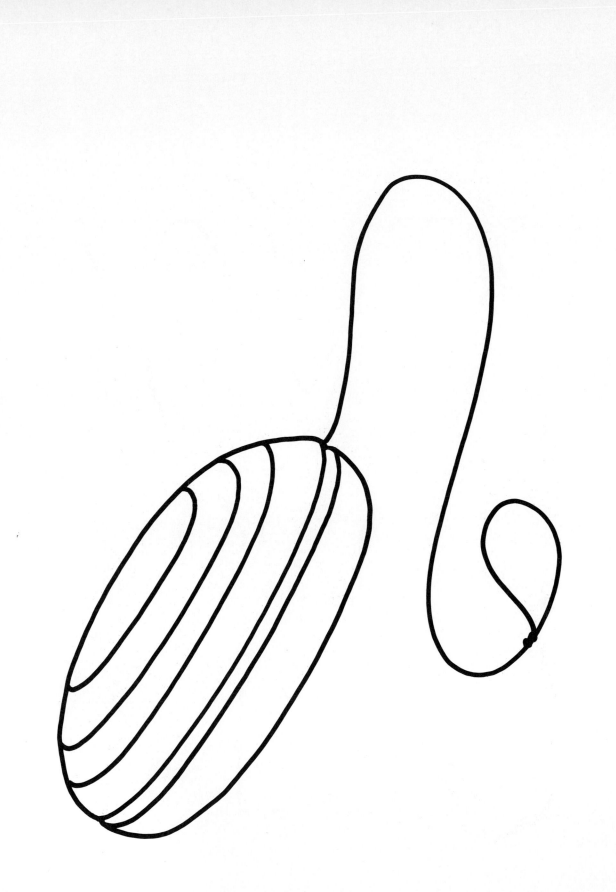

Visual closure card: yo-yo 29

Visual closure card: *Y*/Golden letter 285

Z

z

Z z

zippy zebra (See pattern, page 291.)

Zippy zebras grazed on our chalkboard.

Letter bag items

zebra	zither
zero	zoo
zig zag	zucchini
zinnia	zwieback
zipper	

Multisensory letter projects

zig zag Z

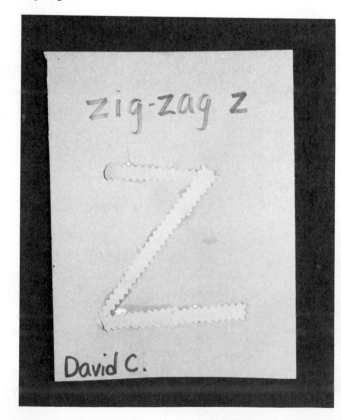

Zigzag *Z* Letter Project

Other projects

zoo pictures

- Have children draw animals. Staple paper fence bars over them.

zucchini prints

zinnias

- Have children fringe two different-sized circles of paper and paste them together.

Thinking skills

Comprehension:

- Have children explore one of the following sets: zucchini, zebras, or zoo animals. Have children touch, smell, and describe each item.

- Help children learn about the care and feeding of animals in zoos and wildlife preserves.

- Use visual closure cards. (See examples, pages 292–293.)
- Provide zippers of different types and sizes for children to use.

Memory:
- Use the memory tray with miniature zoo animals.
- Designate "magic" pages in books that are read.

Decision making:
- Have children classify one of the following sets: zucchini, zebras, or zoo animals. Discuss the classifications.
- Let children pantomime zoo animals.
- Ask children to arrange zippers in sequence from largest to smallest.

Creativity:
- Have children brainstorm zig zag things.

Food projects

zucchini fritters (*Cook and Learn*)
zucchini muffins (*Cook and Learn*)

Books

Animals in the Zoo, illustrated by Feodor Rojankonsky. New York: Alfred A. Knopf, 1962.

We Need a Bigger Zoo, by Eve Bunting, illustrated by Bob Barner. Lexington, Mass.: Ginn, 1974.

Zoophapets, by Robert Tallon. New York: Scholastic Inc., 1979.

Songs and fingerplays

The Zoo
This is the way the elephant goes,
  (Clasp hands and move arms back and forth.)
With curly trunk instead of nose.
The buffalo, all shaggy and fat,
Has two sharp horns in place of hat.
  (Point fingers out from forehead.)

The hippo with his mouth so wide
Lets you see what is inside.
  (Open and close hands to make mouth movements.)
The wiggly snake upon the ground
Crawls along without a sound.
  (Weave hands back and forth.)
But monkey see and monkey do
Is the funniest animal in the zoo.
  (Put thumbs in ears and wiggle hands.)
  –Author unknown–

Science project

Grow zucchini.
- Record the sequence of development.

Field trips and visitors

zoo
zither player

Visual closure card: Z/Golden letter 293

Appendix

More About Structure of Intellect (SOI) Theory

What should be included in the curriculum? How can teachers assign relative emphasis to various thinking skills in order to spend proportionately more time on those that are critical? Most educators have asked similar questions, but few have found satisfactory answers. We want to share our answers to these and other related questions.

We believe that one of the great strengths of our alphabet program is its solid grounding in the theory of Jean Piaget and the theory of the Structure of Intellect (SOI). These theories have enabled us to create a curriculum in which the most important thinking skills are developed. In the introduction to this book, we described briefly our use of these theories; but because most educators are less familiar with the SOI theory than with Piaget's, we will spend additional time explaining the SOI.

The Structure of Intellect (SOI) theory provides an interesting, comprehensive way to think about intelligence. Many of us are accustomed to thinking that intelligence is described by a single number that can be ascertained by a trained psychologist after administering a test. In order to understand the SOI theory, it is useful to explore the consequences of our traditional ideas about intelligence. In the traditional psychometric approach, intelligence is expressed as follows: Suzy has an I.Q. of 120; Miguel has an I.Q. of 135; Angela has an I.Q. of 75; Missy has an I.Q. of 90. We know that Suzy and Miguel are above the statistical average of 100 I.Q. points and that Angela and Missy are below that average. But, if these children are students of ours, can we ascertain what to do after the I.Q. scores are known in order to make instruction more effective for them? The answer is usually negative. Many educators have found that the traditional approach to thinking about intelligence gives little information about how to be helpful in organizing instruction for individuals and groups.

In contrast, the SOI theory deals not only with how much intelligence a student has, but it also describes what kind of intelligence. The SOI model expresses intelligence in terms of five main kinds of abilities rather than in terms of a single number. The SOI theory shows how to understand the intellectual strengths and weaknesses that all people have. What we like best about the SOI approach to intelligence is that it helps us to know how to organize our curriculum in order to *build* intelligence. One of the goals of the SOI theory is to teach children *how to learn.*

The SOI theory was formulated in the 1950s by J. P. Guilford. In the years since then, it has been refined and applied to curriculum by Mary Meeker. The theory grew out of the statistical technique of factor analysis applied to many measures of intelligence. Factor analysis identified separate abilities that students use in their thinking. These separate thinking abilities can provide the foundation for curriculum development. We used our knowledge of the SOI theory in our alphabet program to ensure that we were, indeed, incorporating the whole range of thinking abilities into the curriculum.

The SOI model is often depicted as a three-dimensional cube. One dimension of the cube includes five operations or ways of thinking: comprehension, memory, decision making, problem solving and following directions (convergent production), and creativity (divergent production). These five operations have given structure to our alphabet program. We will briefly define each of the five operations.

Comprehension is the primary process of thinking —the awareness or perception of information in some form. One example of comprehension would follow from a child's experience in carving a pumpkin; new sensations would be made available to that child. (A pumpkin shell is very tough and hard to cut; there are strings and seeds inside, etc.) Unless comprehension takes place, there is nothing for the child to remember, to use as data for decision making, or to think about in more complex ways. As basic as comprehension is, though, educators often neglect opportunities to develop it. Our alphabet program lists a variety of comprehension activities for each letter of the alphabet.

Memory involves the storage of information so that it is available for future use. We use memory when we recall tactile sensations, factual information, and emotional reactions. Well-developed memory skills are vital to success in the educational system and in the world at large. We often observe that people with good memory skills succeed, but there is little help for those with memory deficits. Research has shown memory training to be effective, and we incorporate it into the activities given for all letters.

Decision making builds on comprehension and memory. It includes making choices or judgments about experiences with materials, with information, or with other people. Examples of decision making are choosing what to wear and arranging objects from largest to smallest. The ability to make appropriate, thoughtful judgments develops gradually over time. For each letter of the alphabet, we have organized specific activities to give children practice in making decisions.

Problem solving and following directions involves making an orderly and systematic journey from the statement of a problem to its solution. There are many occasions in education when it is appropriate for students to produce the one best response to a question. It is easy for some students to think in this manner; others need assistance. We have designed the multisensory letter projects, food projects, and other projects to provide the prerequisites for exercising systematic problem-solving strategies.

Creativity is probably the most neglected of the five thinking skills in our educational system. In being creative, people exercise their ability to generate fluent, flexible, original, and elaborate responses to a given set of data. Creativity is used whenever someone comes up with a unique, workable solution to a problem. All individuals have creative potential that can and should be nurtured. Throughout the alphabet program we show respect for children's ideas and beliefs. We have also devised specific activities to enhance creativity.

The other two dimensions to the SOI cube are known as the contents and products of thinking. The four contents of thinking that have been isolated involve the figural (actual objects that can be seen and touched); the symbolic (letters, numbers, or other abstractions); the semantic (words and ideas that carry meaning); and the behavioral (the actions that people take). According to the SOI theory, there are also six products of thinking. These products range from the simplest units (things that can be thought about singly, such as one letter of the alphabet) through more complex classes, relations, systems, transformations, and implications.

Putting all three dimensions of the SOI cube together, specific SOI abilities can be expressed as trigraphs. For instance, visual closure can be expressed as Comprehension of Figural Units (CFU). For those who are interested in the SOI theory, the trigraphs provide a useful shorthand for discussing abilities. For our purposes here, however, we will discuss SOI abilities in terms that are more familiar to most educators.

Research with the SOI model has shown that there are some readiness skills that are critical to success in reading. These readiness skills include the following:*

visual closure

comprehension of similarities of objects

decision making about similarities in objects

classifying objects

memory for individual visual symbols

memory for series of visual symbols

vocabulary of concepts

comprehension of verbal relationships

comprehension of extended verbal information

memory for visual details

word recognition

Development of all these readiness skills is incorporated into our alphabet program. The SOI theory has given us a basis for curriculum development that allows us to meet young children's current and long-term intellectual needs.

For Further Reading

The SOI Theory

Meeker, Mary. *A Beginner's Reader About Guilford's Structure of Intellect.* El Segundo, Calif.: SOI Institute, 1974.

Meeker, Mary. *SOI Techniques: For SOI Questions, For Teaching Competency.* El Segundo, Calif.: SOI Institute, 1981.

Meeker, Mary. *Using SOI Test Results: A Teacher's Guide.* El Segundo, Calif.: SOI Institute, 1981.

---

*Adapted from a list of readiness abilities compiled by Dr. Mary Meeker, SOI Institute, 343 Richmond Street, El Segundo, CA 90245.

Jean Piaget's Theory

Charles, C. M. *Teacher's Petit Piaget.* Belmont, Calif.: Fearon Publishers, 1974.

Labinowicz, Ed. *The Piaget Primer: Thinking, Learning, Teaching.* Menlo Park, Calif.: Addison-Wesley, 1980.

Piaget, Jean, and B. Inhelder. *The Psychology of the Child.* New York: Basic Books, 1969.

Books and Games to Develop SOI Operations

Even if this is your first introduction to the SOI, you have books and materials in your classroom or home that develop SOI thinking skills. To help you to look at your classroom or home in a new way, here are some books and materials that could be used to develop each of the five SOI operations. (Some materials are listed under more than one operation because more than one thinking skill can be involved.)

Comprehension

Books

A, B, See! by Tana Hoban. New York: Greenwillow, 1982.

Each Peach Pear Plum, by Janet and Allan Ahlberg. New York: Scholastic Inc., 1978.

If at First You Do Not See, by Ruth Brown. New York: Holt, Rinehart and Winston, 1982.

Small Worlds Close Up, by Lisa Grillone and Joseph Gennaro. New York: Crown, 1978.

This Can Lick A Lollipop: Body Riddles for Kids, English words by Joel Rothman, Spanish words by Argentina Palacios, photographs by Patricia Ruben. Garden City, N.Y.: Doubleday, 1979.

Materials

Pattern blocks
"Go Fish" or other matching card games
Pattern boards
Dominoes
Bingo cards
Number or alphabet recognition and sequence games
Mazes
Tangrams
Puzzles
Shape recognition games
Dot-to-dot sheets
Matching games
Pick up sticks

Lotto games
Hidden picture books

Memory

Books

Books used to develop memory skills should have a definite sequence that children can be encouraged to recall (for example, *Henny Penny,* by Paul Galdone. New York: Scholastic Inc., 1968).

Materials

Block, bead, or geoboard patterns to be remembered and reproduced
Card games in which memory is required
Concentration games
Recordings of sound patterns to be remembered and reproduced
Rhymes, songs, fingerplays

Decision Making

Books

Books used to develop decision making skills should involve children in making active choices (for example, *Would You Rather . . .,* by John Burningham. New York: Thomas Y. Crowell, 1978).

Materials

Picture sequence cards
Picture or shape classification games
Opposite games
Lotto games
Bingo cards
Puzzles
Collections (buttons, keys, etc.) to classify
Collections to arrange in sequence
Water table and various containers (to explore quantity and conservation)

Problem Solving and Following Directions

Materials

Copying games
Coloring books
Designs or patterns to be reproduced
Sequencing card games
Dominoes
Puzzles
Matching games
Weaving
Lacing
Pattern blocks
Shapes to be traced
Checkers

Science materials: magnets, objects to sink or
  float, objects to vibrate
Recipes for cooking projects

Creativity

Materials

Crayons, paints, etc., used in open-ended ways
Play dough
Blocks
Peg boards and geoboards used in open-ended
  ways
Interlocking blocks
Dramatic play costumes and props
Puppets
Music for movement exploration